the thrifty
cookbook

the thrifty cookbook

More than 80 deliciously easy recipes for households on a budget

RYLAND PETERS & SMALL
LONDON • NEW YORK

Senior Designer Paul Stradling
Senior Editor Abi Waters
Production Manager Gordana Simakovic
Creative Director Leslie Harrington
Editorial Director Julia Charles
Head of Production Patricia Harrington

Indexer Vanessa Bird

First published in 2023
by Ryland Peters & Small
20–21 Jockey's Fields
London WC1R 4BW
and
341 E 11th St
New York, NY 10029

www.rylandpeters.com

10 9 8 7 6 5 4 3 2 1

Text © Miranda Ballard, Susannah Blake, Tamsin
Burnett-Hall, Maxine Clark, Linda Collister, Ross
Dobson, Silvano Franco, Tonia George, Nicola
Graimes, Rachel Anne Hill, Jennifer Joyce, Jenny
Linford, Caroline Marson, Theo A. Michaels, Annie
Nichols, Jane Noraika, Elsa Peterson-Schepelern,
Louise Pickford, Rena Salaman, Jennie Shapter,
Anne Sheasby, Fiona Smith, Linda Tubby, Fran
Warde, Laura Washburn, and Ryland Peters &
Small 2023.
Design and photographs © Ryland Peters & Small
2023.

ISBN: 978-1-78879-525-8

Printed and bound in China.

A CIP record for this book is available from the
British Library and the Library of Congress.

notes

• All spoon measurements are level, unless
otherwise specified.

• Ovens should be preheated to the specified
temperature. Recipes in this book were tested
using a regular oven. If using a fan-assisted
oven, follow the manufacturer's instructions for
adjusting temperatures.

• All eggs are medium, unless otherwise
specified. Recipes containing raw or partially
cooked egg, or raw fish or shellfish, should not
be served to the very young, very old, anyone
with a compromised immune system or
pregnant women.

contents

introduction

Being thrifty is often a matter of common sense and a little forward planning. Get into the habit of keeping your storecupboards stocked with useful basic standbys so that you can whip up a nourishing meal even if you haven't been to the supermarket recently – that will remove the temptation to order in a takeaway.

Buy fresh produce when it's in season, which makes it cheaper because it hasn't been flown around the world; and if it's bought from the market, you may be able to get a good deal on a bag of apples or similar at the end of the day.

Instead of reaching for those chicken fillets on your weekly shop, why not buy drumsticks, thighs, or even a whole chicken, which you can joint and make so much from. Pound for pound, it's much more economical. Rediscover the benefits of cooking with cheaper cuts of meat, which often still have the bone(s) in or are less lean – these cuts need more time to cook but the bones and fat are precisely what makes stews, roasts and pies so tasty and mouth-wateringly tender. This is where weekends can be put to such good use, with slow-cooked dishes designed to be enjoyed both on the day and as leftovers during the week.

Leftovers: such an unappealing word for something with so much potential! If you take just one thing from this book, let it be the value of leftovers. Always think about how you can use up the food lurking in your kitchen before going out to buy more. Hopefully this book will help you make the most of surplus mashed potatoes, rice and spaghetti, and that ever-annoying bowl of egg whites left over from your last dessert recipe.

Thrifty cooking needn't be boring. It's about cutting down on waste (thereby helping the environment), making good use of ingredients and finding new, exciting ways to be frugal.

tips for thrifty cooking

Sometimes you're missing just one ingredient, or have slightly the wrong flour for your recipe. Sometimes you don't have time to cook. Sometimes a dish goes wrong. Don't panic! Here are some tips to guide you through thrifty cooking.

ingredients

• If you have used some eggs for a recipe and are left with unused egg whites or egg yolks, check other recipes to see if they can be used up elsewhere rather than discarded.

• Home-made stock can be frozen in handy portions for future use. Pour the cooled stock into the cups of a non-stick muffin tin and freeze until solid. Remove the frozen blocks from the muffin tin, put them in a freezer bag, seal, label and freeze, Remove stock portions as you need them.

• Make a double quantity of crumble topping (see page 140) and freeze half for next time. Break into small pieces and sprinkle it over the fruit before baking straight from frozen.

• If a recipe calls for snipped fresh chives but you don't have any, try using finely chopped spring onion/scallion.

• Chopped fresh herb stems (such as parsley stalks) are great for adding flavour to soups, sauces and casseroles.

• Keep celery and spring onions/scallions fresh for longer by standing them upright with the root ends in a glass of cold water.

• To keep a fresh loaf of bread crusty, store it in a paper or fabric bag. Wrap bread in foil or in a polythene bag if it has a soft crust.

• An excellent way of thickening soups is to stir in a little oatmeal. It adds flavour and richness too.

• If you run out of self-raising/rising flour, sift together 2 level teaspoons of baking powder with every 225 g/1¾ cups plain/all-purpose flour. This will not create such a high lift as self-raising/rising but it is a good substitute.

• Bulk out pasta or rice salad by adding a can of drained and rinsed beans, such as chickpeas/garbanzo beans, red kidney beans or black-eye beans. Alternatively, add some canned sweetcorn kernels or cooked frozen baby broad/fava beans or peas.

• Add pearl barley to soups or stews to add flavour and texture. It will also create a thickening effect.

• Most vegetables keep best in the refrigerator, but a cool, dark place is also good if you don't have enough fridge space. Potatoes should always be stored in the dark, otherwise they will go green or sprout, making them inedible.

• To yield most juice from a citrus fruit, roll it under the palm of your hand on the work surface first. Citrus fruits at room temperature also yield more fruit.

• When you are getting to the end of packets of breakfast cereal such as cornflakes or bran flakes, crush the bits left with a rolling pin, then store them in an airtight jar and use as an alternative to breadcrumbs, for example coating chicken or fish portions.

using leftovers

• Chop leftover fresh herbs, spoon them into an ice-cube tray, top each portion with a little water and freeze. Once solid, put the cubes in a freezer bag. Seal, label and return to the freezer. Add the frozen herb cubes to soups, casseroles and sauces as needed.

• Cut leftover fresh ginger into slices and freeze in a freezer bag for up to 1 month. Defrost and use as required.

• Use the water in which ham or gammon has been boiled to cook green vegetables, giving them a lovely flavour.

• Make leftover bread into breadcrumbs and store in the freezer for up to 3 months.

• Save the cooking water when boiling or steaming vegetables, and add it to soups, sauces, stocks or gravies for extra flavour.

• Cooked rice is a potential source of food poisoning. Cool leftovers quickly (ideally within an hour), then store in an airtight container in the fridge and use within 24 hours. Always reheat cooked cold rice until piping hot.

• Leftover grated hard cheese freezes well, but soft cheese such as Brie and most blue cheeses (Stilton is an exception) does not. Grated cheese can be used straight from the freezer.

• Freeze leftover wine in an ice-cube tray. Once solid, transfer the wine cubes to a freezer bag. The wine cubes can be added to casseroles, stews and gravies for extra flavour.

• Use pastry trimmings to make biscuits. Gently knead in flavourings such as desiccated coconut and Demerara sugar, finely chopped nuts, chopped herbs and grated cheese, then cut into small shapes and bake in a moderate oven until crisp and golden.

quick fixes

• If you add too much salt to a soup or casserole, add one or two peeled potatoes (cut into chunks) to soak up the salt, then continue to cook until tender. Discard the potatoes before serving.

• To ripen an avocado or fruit such as a hard nectarine or peach, put it in a brown paper bag with a banana and keep at room temperature – ethylene released from the banana will hasten the ripening process.

• If you are melting chocolate and it becomes stiff and grainy, it has been overheated. Take it off the heat and stir in 1–2 teaspoons of vegetable oil, a few drops at the time, until the chocolate is smooth. However, if the chocolate is very scorched it may be unusable.

• If marzipan or almond paste has become hard during storage, seal it in a polythene bag with a slice of fresh bread. The moisture from the bread should restore the marzipan to its pliable state.

• If clear honey (or syrup) hardens during storage, stand the jar in a bowl of hot water for a few minutes or until the honey becomes liquid, rotating the jar occasionally.

• Sometimes moist brown sugar, such as muscovado, becomes hard during storage, due to exposure to air. Add a wedge or two of fresh apple or a slice of fresh bread to the sugar container and the moisture should be restored within a couple of days.

• When baking, use the foil wrappers from blocks of butter or hard margarine to grease cake and loaf tins.

symbols used on recipes

The following symbols have been used to help you identify if a recipe is suitable for your needs:

(V) = Vegetarian

(M) = Meat or Poultry

(F) = Fish

1

budget breakfasts

bircher muesli

This is a type of summer porridge with a texture you either love or hate, but there is definitely something comforting about its soggy sweetness. It will keep for 2–3 days in the fridge, but it is best to leave the apple out so it doesn't brown if you are not eating straight away.

125 g/1 cup rolled oats

75 g/½ cup golden sultanas/ raisins

175 ml/¾ cup pure apple juice

freshly squeezed juice of 1 lemon

100 g/¼ cup natural/plain yoghurt

1 apple, cored, peeled and grated

25 g/3 tablespoons flaked almonds

mixed summer berries, to serve

clear honey, to serve

SERVES 4–6

(V)

Put the oats and sultanas in a large dish. Pour over the apple and lemon juices. Cover with a tea towel and leave to soak overnight. Alternatively, place everything in an airtight container and stick in the fridge, especially if it is very hot.

The next morning when you're ready for breakfast, stir the yoghurt, apple and almonds into the soaked muesli. Divide between 4–6 bowls, scatter some brightly coloured berries over the top and finish with a zigzag of clear honey.

rhubarb compote with yoghurt

Rosewater, like orange flower water, is sold in the baking section of supermarkets, in chemist shops, and in ethnic food stores specializing in Middle Eastern or Indian products. It can be left out if you'd prefer or can't get hold of it though. This dish also works as a refreshing dessert.

500 g/1 lb rhubarb, trimmed

50 g/¼ cup caster/superfine sugar, or to taste

125 g/½ cup natural/plain yoghurt

1 tablespoon clear honey

½ tablespoon rosewater

SERVES 4

V

Cut the rhubarb into 5-cm/2-inch slices and put into a saucepan. Add the sugar and 4 tablespoons water. Bring to the boil, cover and simmer gently for about 15 minutes until the rhubarb has softened. Taste and stir in a little extra sugar if necessary. Transfer to a dish and leave to cool.

Put the yoghurt, honey and rosewater into a bowl, mix well, then serve with the rhubarb.

cinnamon toast

The quickest and thriftiest breakfast treat yet invented – hot buttered toast sprinkled with cinnamon-flavoured sugar, then grilled until crunchy. Thick slices of bread, challah or brioche (two kinds of soft bread) work best, but you can also use crumpets or English muffins split in half.

2 thick slices of white bread

unsalted butter, for spreading

1½ tablespoons caster/superfine sugar

½ teaspoon ground cinnamon

SERVES 1 2

(V)

Preheat the grill/broiler.

Toast the 2 slices of bread in a toaster, then spread all over with butter.

Mix the sugar with the cinnamon, then sprinkle it over the buttered toast to cover in an even layer. Put the toast under the grill for 30 seconds to 1 minute until the sugar has melted and looks bubbly, then carefully remove it.

Leave to cool for a minute (the sugar is very hot and will burn your lips) before eating.

potato, apple & onion hash

The sweetness of the apple together with the subtle nuttiness of the potato and savoury onion makes this simple hash very tasty indeed. Serve it for breakfast or brunch accompanied by bacon or sausages.

500 g/17½ oz. waxy potatoes, peeled

1 tablespoon olive oil

1 onion, sliced

15 g/1 tablespoon butter

1 red-skinned apple, cored and thinly sliced

salt and freshly ground black pepper

freshly chopped parsley, to garnish

SERVES 4

V

Cook the potatoes in boiling, salted water until tender; drain and cut into chunks.

Heat the olive oil in a large frying pan/skillet. Add the onion and fry for 3 minutes, stirring now and then, until softened. Add the potato chunks and fry, stirring often, for around 5 minutes, until lightly browned.

Make a space in the frying pan/skillet and add the butter. Once the butter has melted, add the apple, mixing it with the butter. Fry the mixture for 5 minutes, stirring often, until the apple is lightly browned.

Season with freshly ground black pepper, garnish with parsley and serve at once.

scotch pancakes

Scotch pancakes should be served warm, more or less straight from the pan, spread with butter and sprinkled with sugar.

100 g/¾ cup self-raising/self-rising flour

a pinch of salt

1 egg

25 g/2 tablespoons caster/superfine sugar, plus extra to serve

125 ml/½ cup milk

40 g/3 tablespoons unsalted butter, plus extra to serve

MAKES 12

(V)

Put the flour and salt in a large mixing bowl, make a dip in the centre and add the egg, sugar and milk.

Melt 25 g/2 tablespoons of the butter in a small saucepan, then add to the mixing bowl. Work the mixture together with a whisk or wooden spoon to make a smooth batter. Beat for 1 minute, then set aside for 10 minutes.

Set a frying pan/skillet over medium heat, add the remaining butter and when it melts, swish it around the pan, then pour off the excess into a small heatproof bowl. Put the pan back on the heat and spoon about 1 tablespoon of the batter into the pan. Cook until the pancake browns and bubbles appear on the surface, then turn it over. Transfer to a plate and keep it warm in a low oven while you cook the remainder. Return a little of the melted butter back to the pan as necessary.

Serve immediately, spread with butter and sprinkled with caster sugar.

ham & egg breakfast quesadilla

These breakfast quesadillas are a perfect budget breakfast as you really can use whatever you have to hand in the fridge or cupboard – a great way to make the most of your ingredients.

4 slices thick ham

8 large flour tortillas

200 g/2 cups grated Cheddar cheese

a 400-g/14-oz. can baked beans in tomato sauce

1 tablespoon vegetable oil

4 tablespoons butter

4 large eggs

SERVES 4–6

(M)

Preheat the oven to 120°C (250°F) Gas ½.

To assemble the quesadillas, put a slice of ham on half of the tortillas. Sprinkle each with a quarter of the cheese and spoon over a quarter of the beans. Top each with a plain tortilla.

Heat the oil in a non-stick frying pan/skillet set over medium heat. When hot, add a quesadilla, lower the heat and cook for 2–3 minutes until golden on one side and the cheese begins to melt. Carefully turn over and cook the other side for 2–3 minutes. Transfer to a heatproof plate and keep warm in the preheated oven while you cook the other quesadillas.

Melt 1 tablespoon of the butter in a small non-stick frying pan/skillet. Add an egg and fry until cooked through, turning once to cook both sides if desired. Repeat to cook the remaining eggs.

Cut each quesadilla into wedges and top with a fried egg. Serve immediately while still warm.

bubble & squeak patties

A great way of using up leftover mashed potatoes, these patties are good with grilled tomatoes and sausages. They're also just as nice eaten cold as a snack.

100 g/1 cup shredded Savoy cabbage

250 g/1½ cups cooked mashed potatoes

50 g/¼ cup grated mature/sharp Cheddar

1½ teaspoons Dijon mustard

1 small egg, lightly beaten

plain flour, for dusting

2 tablespoons sunflower/safflower or rapeseed oil

salt and freshly ground black pepper

MAKES 6

V

Steam the cabbage for 2–3 minutes until just tender. Leave to cool, then squeeze out any excess water using your hands. Finely chop the cabbage, then put it in a bowl with the mashed potatoes, cheese and Dijon mustard. Season to taste and mix until combined, then stir in the egg.

Divide the mixture into 6. Using floured hands, form each portion into a flat round shape. Lightly dust each patty with flour.

Pour the oil into a large non-stick frying pan/skillet and heat. Cook 3 patties at a time for 3–4 minutes each side until golden, adding a little more oil if necessary. Remove with a slotted spoon and drain on kitchen paper.

hash browns <small>pictured right</small>

With their delicate, lacy texture and the contrast between crisp edges and yielding, tender centres, hash browns are a budget-friendly treat! Serve them for a leisurely weekend brunch, with slices of roast ham or grilled/broiled bacon and roasted tomatoes.

600 g/21 oz. potatoes, peeled

salt and freshly ground black pepper

clarified butter or sunflower oil, for shallow-frying

freshly chopped parsley, to garnish

MAKES 12

 V or M

Grate the potatoes coarsely and place in a large bowl of cold water for 10 minutes; drain. Wrap the grated potato in a clean kitchen towel and squeeze out the excess moisture. Season with salt and freshly ground black pepper, mixing well.

Add enough clarified butter or oil to form a thin layer in a large frying pan/skillet and heat through. Fry the hash browns in batches. Place four small handfuls of the potato mixture in the frying pan/skillet, spacing them well apart. Use a spatula to press each mound of grated potato down to flatten it out. Fry them until golden brown underneath, then carefully turn over and fry for a few more minutes on the other side. Remove and keep warm.

Repeat the process with the remaining grated potato, making 12 hash browns in all. Garnish with parsley and serve with your choice of ham, tomatoes or homemade baked beans.

frazzled eggs & smoked gammon

The eggs here are fried quickly in very hot oil, giving them an almost lacy look and lovely crisp texture. This has to be one of the quickest and easiest breafasts imaginable and perfect for a weekend brunch.

2 tablespoons wholegrain mustard

1 tablespoon clear honey

4 smoked gammon steaks

2 tablespoons olive oil

4 large eggs

salt and freshly ground black pepper

SERVES 4

(M̄)

Preheat the grill/broiler.

Mix the mustard and honey together and brush over the gammon steaks. Grill for 2–3 minutes on each side, until cooked through. Cover loosely with foil and keep them warm while cooking the eggs.

Heat the oil in a frying pan/skillet until hot. Add the eggs, 2 at a time, and cook until the whites are bubbly and crispy looking. Put an egg on top of each gammon steak. Sprinkle with salt and pepper and serve.

breakfast burrito

This breakfast burrito with its fresh salsa and satisfying guacamole is a fantastic way to start the day.

5 large eggs

1 large potato, cooked and diced

1 fresh red or green chilli/chile, finely chopped

2–3 spring onions/scallions, finely chopped

a small bunch fresh coriander/cilantro, finely chopped

1 teaspoon fine sea salt

2 tablespoons butter

75 g/scant 1 cup grated Cheddar cheese

2 large flour tortillas

1 avocado, thinly sliced

tomato salsa, to serve

SERVES 2

V

Put the eggs in a large bowl and whisk well. Stir in the potato, chilli, spring onions, coriander and salt.

Melt the butter in a large frying pan/skillet. Add the egg mixture and cook, stirring often, until the eggs are just set. Stir in the cheese, cook for 1 minute then transfer to a warmed plate for a moment.

To serve, divide the egg mixture between warmed tortillas and top with avocado slices. Fold the bottom up over most of the filling, then fold over the sides, overlapping to enclose the filling but leaving the burrito open at one end.

Serve immediately with tomato salsa and any excess ingredients on the side.

baked mushroom & egg ramekins

Mushrooms and eggs have a delicious affinity – their delicate flavours complementing each other, rather than overpowering. This traditional egg dish is given a luxurious touch by adding a layer of fried mushrooms. Serve with toast fingers for brunch.

1 tablespoon olive oil

½ onion, finely chopped

400 g/14 oz. white/cup mushrooms, thinly sliced

2 tablespoons any freshly chopped green herb, plus extra to garnish (optional)

4 eggs

4 tablespoons double/heavy cream

4 tablespoons grated Parmesan cheese

salt and freshly ground black pepper

4 ramekins

SERVES 4

(V)

Preheat oven to 180°C (350°F) Gas 4.

Heat the olive oil in a frying pan/skillet. Fry the onion over low heat, until softened. Add the mushrooms, increase the heat, and fry briefly until the mushrooms are softened. Mix in the herbs, if using, season with salt and freshly ground black pepper, and cook for a further 2 minutes.

Divide the mushroom mixture between the 4 ramekin dishes. Break an egg into the centre of each ramekin. Season the eggs with salt and freshly ground black pepper. Pour a tablespoon of cream over each egg, then sprinkle each with Parmesan cheese.

Bake in the preheated oven for 8–10 minutes for runny yolks, or 15–20 minutes for set yolks. Garnish with extra herbs, if using, and serve warm from the oven.

corned beef hash

The British invented bubble and squeak to use up leftovers from a dinner of beef brisket, potato and cabbage. Americans dropped the cabbage and called it corned beef hash – a hearty savoury breakfast dish that is brilliant for using up leftovers.

3 baking potatoes (about 700 g/1½ lbs.), peeled and diced

3 tablespoons butter

1 onion, diced

1 garlic clove, finely chopped

300 g/10 oz. cooked corned beef brisket, diced

½ teaspoon Tabasco sauce

1 tablespoon pure vegetable oil

4 eggs

salt and freshly ground black pepper

SERVES 4

(M)

Boil the potatoes in salted water for about 6 minutes, then drain and put in a large bowl. Heat 1 tablespoon of the butter in a large, heavy frying pan/skillet. Add the onion, garlic and corned beef. Season and sauté for 5 minutes. Pour the mixture into the bowl with the potatoes. Add the Tabasco and mix well.

Add the remaining butter to the frying pan/skillet. Pour the potato mixture into it and press everything down firmly. Cover with a heavy lid or plate that will fit just inside the pan to weight the mixture down. Cook over medium heat for 10 minutes. Turn the mixture over in batches and cook for 10 minutes on the other side. The meat should be brown and crisp; keep cooking and turning if it isn't.

Make 4 indentations in the potatoes and crack an egg into each. Place a fitted lid over the pan and cook until the eggs are done. Alternatively, in a separate non-stick frying pan/skillet, heat 1 tablespoon vegetable oil and fry the eggs. Place one fried egg on top of each serving of corned beef hash. You can also poach the eggs instead of frying them.

baked eggs with smoked salmon & chives

This speedy breakfast can be adapted to use up whatever ingredients you have to hand in the fridge – ham instead of salmon, add some mushrooms and/or tomatoes and whatever herbs you may have lurking to change things up.

200 g/8 oz. smoked salmon slices, chopped

1 tablespoon chopped fresh chives

4 eggs

4 tablespoons/¼ cup double/heavy cream

salt and freshly ground black pepper

toast, to serve

4 ramekins, 200 ml/1 cup each, well buttered

SERVES 4

(F)

Preheat the oven to 180°C (350°F) Gas 4.

Divide the smoked salmon and chives between the 4 buttered ramekins. Make a small indent in the salmon with the back of a spoon and break an egg in the hollow, sprinkle with a little pepper, and spoon the cream over the top.

Put the ramekins in a roasting pan and half fill the pan with boiling water. Bake in the preheated oven for 10–15 minutes until the eggs have just set. Leave to cool for a few minutes, then serve with toast.

2

lunches & light meals

olive oil & garlic bruschetta

This is pared-down simplicity and so easy to make. It beats the likes of doughballs and garlic bread hands down. The most important thing is not to overcook the garlic – it must on no account turn brown. This is great served instead of garlic bread with a selection of salads.

6 tablespoons/1⅓ cup olive oil, plus extra for drizzling

4 large garlic cloves, thinly sliced

a good pinch of chilli/hot red pepper flakes

4 tablespoons/¼ cup freshly chopped parsley (optional)

4 thick slices of country bread, preferably sourdough

SERVES 4

(V)

Heat a small pan, pour in the olive oil and stir in the garlic. Cook until the garlic starts to give off its aroma and is golden but not brown (or it will taste bitter). Remove from the heat, then mix in the chilli/pepper flakes and parsley, if using. Cover to keep warm.

To make the bruschetta, grill/broil, toast or pan-grill the bread on both sides until lightly charred or toasted, then drizzle with olive oil. Spoon or brush over the garlicky chilli oil.

tomato & garlic bruschetta

Traditionally, this Italian peasant dish is just a slice of bread grilled over hot coals, rubbed with garlic and drizzled with olive oil. The ripe tomato is just crushed in your hand and smashed onto the bread, then eaten immediately. This is bruschetta at its simplest and best. This version is more civilized, but you should try the real thing – it's great fun!

4 large, very ripe tomatoes

4 thick slices of country bread, preferably sourdough

2 garlic cloves, halved

olive oil, for drizzling

salt and freshly ground black pepper

SERVES 4

(V)

Roughly chop the tomatoes and season with salt and pepper.

To make the bruschetta, grill/broil, toast or pan-grill the bread on both sides until lightly charred or toasted. Rub the top side of each slice with the cut garlic, then drizzle with olive oil.

Spoon the tomatoes over the bruschetta and drizzle with more olive oil.

pea, smoked ham & mint soup

Frozen or fresh peas make a very satisfying sweet and savoury base for a soup. If you are into podding your own peas from the garden, the results will be even better, but frozen peas pulled out of the freezer are just as good for a thrifty standby supper.

3 tablespoons olive oil

6 spring onions/scallions, chopped

2 garlic cloves, sliced

200 g/6½ oz. thick slices of smoked ham, finely chopped

10 g/small handful fresh mint, leaves only, or 1 teaspoon dried mint

500 g/1 lb. peas (defrosted or fresh)

1 litre/1 quart hot chicken or vegetable stock

salt and freshly ground black pepper

SERVES 4

(M)

Heat the olive oil in a large saucepan over low heat and add the spring onions. Cook for 2–3 minutes, then add the garlic, ham and half the mint and cook for a further 2 minutes, stirring.

Stir in the peas and pour in the hot stock. Simmer for 2–3 minutes until the peas are tender.

Transfer a third of the soup to a blender and liquidize until completely smooth. Pour back into the soup and mix until amalgamated. Season with just a little salt (the ham will be quite salty already) and some black pepper. Add the remaining mint. Serve with more black pepper.

chicken avgolemono

pictured left

A light, lemony Greek soup – perfect for using up leftover cooked chicken.

1.4 litres/6 cups hot chicken stock

100 g/½ cup long-grain rice

400 g/14 oz. cooked chicken, shredded

3 eggs

juice of 1 lemon

freshly chopped flat-leaf parsley, to serve

croutons, to serve

SERVES 4

M

Heat the stock in a large saucepan and add the rice. Bring to the boil and simmer for 15 minutes or until the rice is tender. Add the chicken and warm through for 2–3 minutes.

In the meantime, whisk the eggs with the lemon juice in a small bowl. Add a ladleful of the warm stock and whisk until thinned.

Remove the soup from the heat and gradually pour in the egg mixture, whisking to amalgamate it. It should thicken in the residual heat, but if you need to, place it over low heat for just 3–4 minutes, stirring the bottom of the pan to thicken. Do not return to high heat once the egg has been added, or it will boil and scramble.

Serve garnished with parsley and croutons.

chicken noodle soup

You really need a deep, flavoursome base for the ultimate chicken noodle soup so this is best made with home-made chicken stock for the most flavour. However, a stock made from a cube will also work for a super-quick dish.

1 tablespoon olive oil

1 onion, chopped

2 large carrots, chopped

2 celery sticks, thickly sliced

1 litre/1 quart hot chicken stock

90 g/3 oz. fine egg noodles, broken into pieces

leftovers from a roasted chicken, pulled off the carcass

a small handful of fresh flat-leaf parsley, finely chopped

salt and freshly ground black pepper

SERVES 4

M

Heat the olive oil in a saucepan. Add the onion, carrots and celery, and season. Sauté for 5 minutes, then pour in the stock. Bring to the boil and add the noodles. Cook until the noodles are al dente.

Chop up the chicken meat, then add to the saucepan. Sprinkle in the chopped parsley, season to taste and serve.

tomato soup

Keep this simple with the reddest, ripest tomatoes you can find. Or you can pep it up with a dollop of flavoursome pesto on top before serving if you have any to hand.

1 kg/2 lbs. very ripe red tomatoes

500 ml/2 cups hot chicken stock, or to taste

salt and freshly ground black pepper

to serve (optional)

grated zest and juice of 1 unwaxed lemon

4 tablespoons/¼ cup pesto

freshly snipped chives or torn basil

SERVES 4

M or V

To skin the tomatoes, cut a cross in the base of each and dunk into a saucepan of boiling water. Remove after 10 seconds and put into a strainer set over a large saucepan. Slip off and discard the skins and cut the tomatoes in half around their 'equators'. Using a teaspoon, deseed into the strainer, then press the pulp and juice through the strainer and add to the blender. Discard the seeds. Chop the tomato halves and add to the blender.

Purée the tomatoes, adding a little of the stock to help the process – you may have to work in batches. Add the remaining stock, season to taste and transfer to the saucepan. Heat well without boiling.

Serve topped with a spoonful of lemon juice, grated lemon zest, pesto, chives or basil, if using, and a little more black pepper.

mixed bean soup pictured left

Using canned beans, this soup takes no time at all to prepare.

1 tablespoon olive oil

3 large garlic cloves, 2 cut into slices, 1 crushed

1 large onion, finely chopped

250 g/1 heaping cup Puy lentils

1 litre/1 quart boiling chicken or vegetable stock, plus extra to taste

100 g/½ cup canned butter beans

200 g/1 cup canned green flageolet beans

200 g/1 cup canned red kidney beans

200 g/1 cup canned haricot or cannellini beans

salt and freshly ground black pepper

fresh parsley or basil

SERVES 4

(V) or (M)

Heat the oil in a frying pan/skillet, add the sliced garlic and fry gently on both sides until crisp and golden. Remove and drain on kitchen paper.

Add the onion and crushed garlic to the frying pan/skillet, adding extra oil if necessary, and cook gently until softened and transparent. Add the lentils and half the boiling stock and cook until the lentils are just tender.

Meanwhile, rinse and drain all the beans. Put them in a sieve and dunk the sieve in a large saucepan of boiling water. The beans are cooked – you are just reheating them.

Add the hot beans to the lentils and add the remaining stock. Season to taste. If the soup is too thick, add boiling stock or water. Ladle into bowls, top with the reserved fried garlic and herbs and serve with crusty bread.

chickpea, lemon & mint soup

This storecupboard-based soup couldn't be easier. It's made from a minimal number of ingredients, but has an intriguingly complex flavour.

1.2 kg canned/3 x 14-oz. cans chickpeas/ garbanzo beans

2 garlic cloves, crushed

grated zest and juice of 2 unwaxed lemons

3 tablespoons freshly chopped mint

2 tablespoons olive oil

salt and freshly ground black pepper

SERVES 4

(V)

Drain the liquid from the chickpeas into a jug, and make up to 750 ml/3 cups with water.

Tip two-thirds of the drained chickpeas into a food processor and add the garlic, lemon zest and juice, mint, olive oil and enough of the chickpea liquid to blend to a purée.

Pour into a saucepan and stir in the remaining whole chickpeas and liquid. Season to taste and heat through for about 5 minutes until gently bubbling. Ladle into bowls and serve immediately.

Swiss chard & white bean soup

This minestrone-type soup is beefed up by serving it over thick and garlicky toast to soak up all the goodness.

2 tablespoons unsalted butter

1 onion, chopped

a small bunch of Swiss chard (about 350 g/12 oz.), finely chopped

400 g/14 oz. canned cannellini beans, drained but not rinsed

1 litre/1 quart hot vegetable stock

4 thick slices of toast

2 garlic cloves, halved

olive oil, for drizzling

salt and freshly ground black pepper

grated Parmesan, to serve

SERVES 4

(V)

Melt the butter in a saucepan over medium heat. Add the onion and cook for 4–5 minutes to soften. Add the chard and cook for 5 minutes, stirring, until softened.

Mash the beans with a fork, then add to the saucepan with the stock and gently bring to the boil. Season.

Rub the toast with the cut side of the garlic, then place each one in a serving bowl. Drizzle each piece of bread with olive oil and ladle over the soup. Sprinkle the Parmesan on top and serve immediately.

rice noodle salad with prawns

A delicious and filling lunch. If you'd like to spice it up a bit, add some chopped spring onions/scallions, fresh coriander/cilantro and red chilli/chile if you have any to use up.

150 g/5 oz. thin rice noodles

2 tablespoons vegetable oil

1 cm/½ inch fresh ginger, peeled and finely chopped

1 garlic clove, crushed

175 g/6 oz. cooked peeled prawns/shrimp

50 g/2 oz. fine green beans, trimmed

1 carrot, cut into matchsticks

juice of ½ a lime

50 g/¼ cup cashew nuts, chopped

1 tablespoon sesame seeds, lightly toasted in a dry frying pan/skillet

SERVES 6

(F)

Cook the noodles according to the packet instructions. Drain, toss them in a little of the oil and leave to cool in the colander for 10 minutes.

Heat the remaining oil in a wok or large frying pan/skillet and add the ginger, garlic, prawns/shrimp, beans and carrot. Cook over medium heat for 4 minutes, stirring constantly.

Add the mixture to the cooled noodles and mix well. Sprinkle with cashew nuts and toasted sesame seeds.

spicy halloumi & chickpeas

Halloumi has a reasonably long shelf-life before it is opened, which means you can keep a pack tucked away in the fridge. Harissa is a fiery paste – see Note below to make your own.

1 tablespoon olive oil

1 onion, finely chopped

1 garlic clove, crushed

1 tablespoon harissa paste (see Note below)

400 g/14 oz. canned chickpeas/garbanzo beans, drained

400 g/14 oz. canned chopped tomatoes

125 g/4 oz. halloumi cheese, cubed

100 g/2 cups baby spinach

juice of ½ lemon

salt and black pepper

grated Parmesan, to serve

SERVES 2

V

Put the oil into a large saucepan and gently sauté the onion and garlic until softened. Add the harissa paste, chickpeas and chopped tomatoes. Bring to the boil and simmer for about 5 minutes.

Add the halloumi cheese and spinach, cover and cook over low heat for a further 5 minutes. Season to taste and stir in the lemon juice. Spoon onto serving plates and sprinkle with the Parmesan cheese. Serve immediately with a crisp green side salad.

Note: If you don't have harissa paste, you can make your own by mixing together ½ teaspoon cayenne pepper, 1 tablespoon ground cumin, 1 tablespoon tomato purée/paste and the juice of 1 lime.

couscous tabbouleh

pictured right

Using cold water to hydrate couscous allows it to fluff up but still retain an al dente texture. Using couscous in a dish like this means you get all the fresh crispness of a salad, but with the sustaining benefits of a grain.

75 g/⅓ cup couscous

4 spring onions/scallions, finely chopped

⅓ cucumber, diced

3 tomatoes (about 300 g/10 oz.), deseeded and diced

a large handful of fresh flat-leaf parsley, finely chopped

a small handful of fresh mint, finely chopped

lemon dressing

juice of 1 lemon

1 garlic clove, crushed

3 tablespoons olive oil

salt and freshly ground black pepper

SERVES 4

V

Put the couscous in a bowl with 250 ml/⅓ cup cold water – enough to make the couscous just moist rather than saturated. Leave for 10 minutes or until fluffy. When ready, stir in the spring onions/scallions, cucumber, tomatoes, parsley and mint.

To make the lemon dressing, put the lemon juice, garlic and olive oil in a bowl and whisk with a fork. Stir into the salad, add salt and pepper to taste, then serve.

Tuscan tomato & bread salad

This is the perfect thrifty salad – make it when you have the reddest, over-ripe tomatoes and day-old stale bread to use up.

6 very ripe tomatoes

2 garlic cloves, sliced

4 thick slices of day-old bread

about 10 cm/4 inches cucumber, halved, deseeded and thinly sliced

1 red onion, chopped

1 tablespoon freshly chopped flat-leaf parsley

8–12 tablespoons olive oil

2 tablespoons white wine vinegar or cider vinegar

a handful of fresh basil leaves, torn

4 tablespoons/¼ cup capers packed in brine, rinsed and drained

salt and freshly ground black pepper

SERVES 4

Preheat the oven to 180°C (350°F) Gas 4.

Cut the tomatoes in half, spike with slivers of garlic and roast in the preheated oven for about 1 hour, or until wilted and some of the moisture has evaporated.

Meanwhile, put the bread on an oiled stove-top griddle pan and cook until lightly toasted and barred with grill marks on both sides. Tear or cut the toast into pieces and put into a salad bowl. Sprinkle with a little water until damp. Add the tomatoes, cucumber, onion, parsley, salt and pepper. Sprinkle with the olive oil and vinegar, toss well, then set aside for about 1 hour to develop the flavours.

Add the basil leaves and capers and serve.

French toast & fried tomatoes

Who says French toast is just for breakfast? Topping it with fried tomatoes makes a juicy, tasty snack. Frying tomatoes seems to intensify their flavour and the heat makes them soft and velvety – truly delicious on eggy bread.

4 eggs

4 tablespoons/¼ cup milk

4 slices of bread

50 g/4 tablespoons butter

4 ripe tomatoes, halved

salt and freshly ground black pepper

SERVES 4

(V)

Beat together the eggs and milk in a large, shallow dish and add some salt and pepper. Add the bread and leave to soak for 5 minutes on each side so that all the egg mixture is absorbed.

Heat a large, non-stick frying pan/skillet over medium heat. Add the soaked bread and cook over medium-low heat for 3–4 minutes on each side.

In a separate pan, melt the butter. Add the tomatoes and fry on each side for 2 minutes, then serve on top of the hot French toast.

smoked mackerel & bulgur wheat salad

The creamy horseradish dressing is a fabulous complement to the richness of the smoked mackerel in this salad, while raw vegetables add crunch and colour.

60 g/½ cup bulgur wheat

1 tablespoon lemon juice

1 tablespoon freshly snipped chives

½ yellow (bell) pepper, deseeded and diced

8 radishes, sliced

75 g/1½ cups spinach

150 g/5 oz. smoked mackerel fillets, flaked

freshly ground black pepper

dressing

3 tablespoons fromage frais/ sour cream

2 teaspoons horseradish sauce

1 teaspoon freshly snipped chives

SERVES 2

(F)

Cook the bulgur wheat in a saucepan of lightly salted boiling water for 15 minutes or until tender. Drain, then mix with the lemon juice, chives, yellow (bell) pepper and radishes.

Divide the spinach leaves between 2 shallow salad bowls, spoon the bulgur wheat on top, then add the flaked smoked mackerel.

Mix the dressing ingredients together and drizzle over the fish. Finish with black pepper.

tuna & bean salad

You can usually make this when you come home from work, all the shops have shut, and you've run out of almost everything. Though not quite as good, you can replace the cannellini beans with chickpeas/garbanzo beans, lentils, borlotti/pinto beans and green flageolets, and even use canned salmon instead of tuna.

1–2 fat garlic cloves, crushed

1 tablespoon sherry vinegar or white wine vinegar

6 tablespoons/⅓ cup olive oil

600 g/1¼ lbs. cooked or canned cannellini beans, rinsed and drained

2 red onions, thinly sliced into petals (and blanched to take the sharp edge off), or 6 small spring onions/scallions, sliced

400 g/14 oz. canned tuna

salt and freshly ground black pepper

a handful of fresh basil leaves, torn

SERVES 6

(F)

Put the garlic on a chopping board, crush with the flat of a knife, add a large pinch of salt, then mash to a paste with the tip of the knife. Transfer to a bowl, add the vinegar and 2 tablespoons of the oil and beat with a fork.

Add the beans and onions and toss gently. Taste, then add extra oil and vinegar to taste.

Drain the tuna and separate into large chunks. Add to the bowl and turn gently to coat with the dressing. Top with the basil and some black pepper.

fresh fried trout

You might feel that having a whole fish for dinner is not the route to thriftiness, but trout can be very inexpensive and this Spanish-inspired recipe uses few ingredients to excellent effect. You can eat it either hot or cold.

3 tablespoons olive oil

150 g/4 oz. bacon lardons or cubed ham

2 trout, cleaned

2 tablespoons plain/all-purpose flour, seasoned with salt and pepper

1 garlic clove, cut into slivers

2 tablespoons freshly chopped flat-leaf parsley

salt and freshly ground black pepper

1 lemon, cut into wedges, to serve

SERVES 2

Heat 1 tablespoon of the oil in a frying pan/skillet, add the bacon and fry until just golden. Remove to a plate.

Dust the fish with the seasoned flour. Open the bellies, season with salt and pepper and put in the garlic slivers.

Heat the remaining oil in the frying pan/skillet, add the trout and fry for 3 minutes on each side. Lower the heat and cook for a further 2 minutes on each side.

Transfer to hot plates, then return the bacon to the pan to warm through. Spoon the bacon on top of the trout and sprinkle with parsley and pepper. Serve hot with lemon wedges, or leave until cold.

mozzarella & tuna quesadilla

Satisfyingly moreish, this golden tortilla parcel is filled with melted mozzarella and tuna. Diced sweet (bell) pepper, chopped spring onions/scallions, or herbs, such as chives, can also be added, if you have any to use up in the fridge.

olive oil, for brushing

2 large soft wheat flour tortillas

100 g/3½ oz. canned tuna, drained and mashed with a fork

6 slices of mozzarella, about 75 g/2½ oz. total weight

10 fresh basil leaves

freshly ground black pepper

SERVES 2–4

(F)

Lightly brush a large non-stick frying pan/skillet with oil. Put one tortilla into the pan so it fits snugly. Spoon the tuna over the tortilla, leaving a 2-cm/1-inch gap around the edge. Top the tuna with the mozzarella and basil, then season with pepper to taste.

Put the second tortilla on top of the filling, pressing it down around the edges. Put the pan over medium-low heat and cook the quesadilla for 3 minutes until the tortilla is golden and beginning to crisp.

To cook the other side of the quesadilla, put a large plate on top of the frying pan/skillet and carefully flip it over to release the quesadilla onto the plate, then slide it back into the pan. Cook the tortilla for another 3 minutes until golden and the mozzarella is melted. Slice into 6 wedges and serve.

cheat's mini pizzas

These ultra-quick pizzas are the answer to fast food when faced with mates so hungry they simply can't wait for the real thing. Passata is just shop-bought sieved tomatoes – perfect as an instant tomato sauce, but if you have canned chopped tomatoes or even jarred tomato sauce left over from last night's pasta, that will do too. Top the pizzas with anything you like!

4 English muffins

150 g/⅔ cup passata (sieved tomatoes)

toppings of your choice, such as diced ham, pineapple, sweetcorn/corn kernels, flaked tuna, sliced mushrooms, (bell) peppers and shredded fresh herbs, etc.

50 g/½ cup mozzarella or Cheddar, grated

SERVES 4

Preheat the oven to 200°C (400°F) Gas 6.

Slice the muffins in half horizontally. Spread the passata over them, then top with any toppings of your choice, or simply with a little grated cheese.

Bake in the preheated oven for 8–10 minutes until the muffins are crispy round the edges and the cheese is golden and bubbling.

lemony mushrooms on toast

This may just be mushroooms on toast, but sometimes the simplest things are the best. Keeping the number of ingredients low helps to keep the cost down per meal. Try to use meaty field/cremini mushrooms here, as they keep their shape best when cooked.

2 tablespoons olive oil

2 dried bay leaves

2 strips of lemon zest

500 g/1 lb. large, flat field mushrooms, thinly sliced

2 garlic cloves, sliced

1 handful of fresh flat-leaf parsley, chopped

1 tablespoon lemon juice

4 slices of sourdough bread, lightly toasted

salt and freshly ground black pepper

SERVES 4

Put the oil in a frying pan/skillet and set it over high heat. Add the mushrooms and cook for 8–10 minutes, turning them often.

Add the bay leaves and lemon zest to the pan and cook for 1 minute to just flavour the mushrooms. Add the garlic and parsley, stir and cook for 1 minute, making sure that the garlic does not burn. Add the lemon juice and season well.

Spoon the mushroom mixture onto the slices of toasted sourdough bread and serve immediately.

tuna pasta salad

This is a good idea for a hurried lunch, but it's also ideal for making in advance and popping in a container for lunch later on to save spending money on lunch out.

100 g/3½ oz. dried pasta, such as penne

1 red onion, thinly sliced

3 celery stalks, chopped

1 carrot, grated

50 g/¼ cup sultanas/raisins

8-cm/3-inch piece of cucumber, chopped

50 g/¼ cup canned sweetcorn/corn kernels

400 g/14 oz. canned tuna, drained and flaked

6 tablespoons/⅓ cup mayonnaise

6 tablespoons/⅓ cup Greek yoghurt

salad leaves/greens

225 g/8 oz. cherry tomatoes, halved

SERVES 4–6

Cook the pasta in a large saucepan of boiling water for 12–15 minutes, or according to the manufacturer's instructions, until al dente. Drain, refresh under cold running water and transfer to a large bowl.

Cut the onion slices in half to form half moons, then add to the bowl along with the celery, carrot, sultanas, cucumber, sweetcorn and tuna.

Mix the mayonnaise with the yoghurt and add it to the salad. Stir gently until well coated. (You can make the recipe up to this point and store, covered, in the refrigerator for up to 2 days.)

To serve, line a plate with salad leaves, put a serving of the pasta salad on top and scatter over a few halved tomatoes.

tuna melt

This is the ultimate tuna melt. Use any kind of white bread – crusty rustic sourdough, a large bloomer or a simple sandwich loaf – just make sure the slices are large and thick.

200 g/6 oz. canned tuna, drained

3–3½ tablespoons mayonnaise

½ tablespoon capers, rinsed and finely chopped

2 small gherkins or 1 large dill pickle in sweet vinegar, diced fairly finely

¼ red (bell) pepper, diced finely

1 tablespoon chopped fresh tarragon (optional)

2 large, thick slices of white crusty bread

4 large, thin slices Swiss cheese, such as Gruyère or Emmenthal

freshly ground black pepper

SERVES 2

(F)

Put the tuna in a bowl and flake the flesh. Add the mayonnaise, capers, gherkins, (bell) peppers and tarragon (if using) and mix well. Season with pepper.

Preheat the grill/broiler.

Toast the bread on one side under the grill/broiler, then turn it over and spread the tuna thickly on the uncooked side. Put 2 cheese slices on top of each toast and grill for about 5 minutes until the cheese is golden and bubbling.

Note: Look for tuna canned in water rather than brine as the capers are salty enough already.

pepperoni, red pepper & crouton frittata

A frittata is Italy's version of an open omelette and it wins hands down as one of the most convenient ways to use up leftovers. This one is packed with tasty chargrilled/roasted (bell) peppers and pepperoni, and must be served straight away, otherwise it goes on cooking and loses its soft creaminess. It can also be left to cool, cut into wedges and enjoyed as part of a lunch-on-the-go the following day.

4 eggs, beaten

25 g/1 oz. Gruyère cheese, grated

1 spring onion/scallion, thinly sliced

25 g/2 tablespoons unsalted butter

50 g/2 oz. firm white bread, torn into small pieces

1 garlic clove, crushed

1 chargrilled/roasted red (bell) pepper, cut into strips

25 g/1 oz. pepperoni, sliced

salt and freshly ground black pepper

a medium sized, ovenproof frying pan/skillet

SERVES 2

(M)

Break the eggs into a bowl and beat well using a fork. Season well and add half the cheese and spring onion/scallion. Mix well.

Melt half the butter in the ovenproof frying pan/skillet. Add the bread pieces and toss them for 2–3 minutes over high heat until golden brown and crispy. Remove from the heat and set aside.

Preheat the grill/broiler.

Add the remaining butter and the garlic to the pan, and when the butter starts to froth, add the beaten eggs. Turn the heat down and leave the eggs to cook gently for a few minutes. Arrange the pepperoni and (bell) pepper strips on the top and sprinkle with the remaining cheese and reserved croutons. Put the frying pan/skillet under the preheated grill/broiler and cook for a further 2–3 minutes until the frittata is puffed and just set but still wobbly. Remove from the grill/broiler and serve immediately with a crisp green salad or a tomato and basil salad.

Variation: Also delicious made with any combination of the following: crumbled firm goats' cheese, sliced mushrooms, baby spinach leaves, courgettes/zucchini or sliced cooked potatoes.

sun-dried tomato frittata

If you have the time, it is worth mixing the tomatoes and sage into the eggs an hour before cooking for a more intense flavour to make the most of your ingredients.

6 large eggs, beaten

8 sun-dried tomatoes in oil, drained and sliced

1 tablespoon freshly chopped sage leaves

50 g/⅓ cup stoned/pitted black olives, thickly sliced

50 g/½ cup Parmesan, grated

2 tablespoons olive oil

1 onion, halved and sliced

salt and freshly ground black pepper

a 20-cm/8-inch ovenproof frying pan/skillet

SERVES 2–3

(V)

Put the eggs, sun-dried tomatoes, sage, black olives, grated Parmesan and some seasoning in a bowl and mix gently.

Heat the oil in the frying pan/skillet, add the onion and cook over low heat until soft and golden. Increase the heat to medium, pour the egg mixture into the pan and stir just long enough to mix in the onion. Cook over medium-low heat until the base of the frittata is golden and the top has almost set.

Preheat the grill/broiler.

Slide the pan under the grill to finish cooking or put a plate on top of the pan and invert the pan. Slide the tortilla back into the pan, brown side up, and cook for 1–2 minutes until lightly browned underneath.

chickpea tortilla

Chickpeas/garbanzo beans are a delicious alternative to potato in a Spanish tortilla, adding a sweet, nutty flavour.

5 large eggs

½ teaspoon Spanish smoked paprika

3 tablespoons freshly chopped flat-leaf parsley

3 tablespoons olive oil

1 large onion, finely chopped

1 red (bell) pepper, halved, deseeded and chopped

2 garlic cloves, finely chopped

400 g/14 oz. canned chickpeas/garbanzo beans, rinsed and well drained

salt and freshly ground black pepper

a 20-cm/8-inch heavy non-stick frying pan/skillet

SERVES 2–3

V

Break the eggs into a large bowl, add salt, pepper and paprika and whisk briefly with a fork. Stir in the chopped parsley.

Heat 2 tablespoons of the oil in the frying pan/skillet. Add the onion and red pepper and cook for about 5 minutes until softened, turning frequently. Add the garlic and chickpeas and cook for 2 minutes. Transfer to the bowl of eggs and stir gently. Add the remaining oil to the pan and return to the heat. Add the chickpea mixture, spreading it evenly in the pan. Cook over medium-low heat until the bottom is golden brown and the top almost set.

Put a plate on top of the frying pan/skillet and invert the pan. Slide the tortilla back into the pan, brown side up, and cook for 2–3 minutes until lightly browned underneath.

field mushroom tortilla

Use up some leftover boiled potatoes in this simple tortilla.

20 g/1½ tablespoons unsalted butter

2 tablespoons olive oil

3 cooked potatoes, diced

200 g/6½ oz. flat field mushrooms

1 garlic clove, crushed

125 g/4 oz. baby spinach

4 eggs

100 ml/⅓ cup milk

salt and freshly ground black pepper

a medium-sized, ovenproof frying pan/skillet

SERVES 4–6

V

Heat the butter and olive oil in the frying pan/skillet, add the potatoes and brown on all sides. Transfer to a plate, then cook the mushrooms on both sides for 5 minutes, adding a little more oil or butter if necessary. Transfer to another plate and return the potatoes to the pan. Sprinkle in the garlic, then add the mushrooms and spinach.

Mix the eggs and milk together, season and pour into the pan. Cover and cook gently for 5 minutes.

Preheat the grill/broiler to medium-high.

Put the tortilla under the grill/broiler for 6–8 minutes, or until golden on top.

bang bang chicken

This is a fantastic salad that's quite unusual and makes a more filling meal than your average leafy green salad – ready-cooked smoked or 'plain-roast' chicken is arranged on sticks of cucumber, then topped with a creamy peanut butter dressing.

400 g/14 oz. ready-cooked boneless chicken, such as smoked chicken, cold roast chicken or cold turkey

1 large carrot, peeled

salad leaves/greens such as crispy iceberg lettuce or Chinese leaves, about 75 g/ 1 cup

1 cucumber, cut into matchsticks

bang bang dressing

5 tablespoons crunchy peanut butter

1 spring onion/scallion, thinly sliced

1 teaspoon sesame oil

1 teaspoon light soy sauce

1 teaspoon caster/superfine sugar

1 teaspoon Chinese white rice vinegar or cider vinegar

3 tablespoons hot water

SERVES 4

(M)

Remove any skin from the chicken and discard. Pull or cut the chicken into shreds the size of your little finger, then put onto a plate.

Make carrot ribbons by 'peeling' the carrot with a vegetable peeler to make ultra-thin long strips of carrot.

Tear any large salad leaves into bite-sized pieces. Arrange the leaves on a serving dish. Scatter the cucumber sticks and carrot ribbons over the leaves. Lastly, arrange the chicken on the top.

To make the bang bang dressing, put the peanut butter in a small bowl with the spring onion. Add the sesame oil, soy sauce, sugar, vinegar, 1 teaspoon cold water and the hot water to the bowl. Stir gently until well mixed. Taste the dressing – it should be a happy balance of salty, sweet and sour flavours, so add more vinegar, sugar or soy as you think is needed. The dressing should be just thin enough to spoon over the chicken, so if it is too thick stir in another tablespoon or so of hot water.

When the sauce seems perfect, spoon it over the chicken and serve.

3

everyday dinners

chopped liver with zhoug

Chopped liver makes a simple, budget-friendly pâté – perfect served with zhoug, a traditional Jewish fresh herb salsa.

4 tablespoons/¼ cup olive oil

1 onion, chopped

500 g/1 lb. chicken livers, cleaned and trimmed

4 hard-boiled eggs, peeled

salt and freshly ground black pepper

sweet paprika and matzo crackers, to serve

zhoug

1 teaspoon cumin seeds

4 large mild green chillies/chiles, deseeded and chopped

8 tablespoons/½ cup freshly chopped flat-leaf parsley

8 tablespoons/½ cup freshly chopped coriander/cilantro

1 garlic clove, chopped

125 ml/½ cup olive oil

SERVES 4–6

(M)

To make the zhoug, heat a small frying pan/skillet and toast the cumin seeds for 30 seconds until fragrant. Remove from the heat and crush with a pestle and mortar. Put in a small food processor with the chillies, parsley, coriander and garlic and blend to a rough paste, adding the olive oil slowly as you do so. Season. Store, chilled, in an airtight container for up to 2 weeks.

Heat 2 tablespoons of the olive oil in a large frying pan/skillet and sauté the onion for 6 minutes, or until soft and pale golden. Set aside.

Season the livers. Heat 1 tablespoon of the oil over high heat and cook half the livers for 3–4 minutes. Set aside and cook the remaining livers. Finely chop the livers and eggs and combine with the onion, then season. Transfer to a dish and sprinkle with paprika. Serve with zhoug and matzo crackers.

fried meatballs

These meatballs are a Greek recipe and made lighter than other meatballs with the addition of soaked bread, which in turn stretches the ingredients further making it a cost-effective meal for a family. Serve with rice.

3 slices of bread (crusts discarded), soaked in water

500 g/1¼ lb. minced/ground beef or lamb

1 tablespoon lemon juice or white wine

1 onion, grated

1 egg, lightly beaten

1 tablespoon dried oregano

a handful of fresh mint, chopped

5 tablespoons plain/all-purpose flour

4–5 tablespoons sunflower/safflower oil

salt and freshly ground black pepper

MAKES 15

(M)

Drain the bread and squeeze out the excess water, then put the bread in a bowl. Add the beef or lamb, lemon juice, onion, egg, oregano, mint, salt and pepper. Mix it with your fingers until well amalgamated.

Put the flour on a work surface. Make round, walnut-sized balls of the mince mixture, then roll them lightly in the flour. If you prefer, you can make them bigger, then flatten them – this will make frying quicker.

Heat the oil in a non-stick frying pan/skillet, add the meatballs and fry, turning them around until golden on all sides and cooked through. Remove and drain on kitchen paper, then serve immediately.

lime pickle & vegetable biryani

Here is a speedy recipe in which vegetables are stir-fried with a spicy curry paste and cooked rice is then added. With the addition of a dollop of the lime pickle that is probably lurking at the back of your fridge, this is a stir-fry with a difference.

2 tablespoons bottled lime pickle

1 onion, chopped

2 garlic cloves

2 teaspoons grated fresh ginger

2 tablespoons olive oil

2 carrots, cut into matchsticks

2 courgettes/zucchini, cut into matchsticks

370 g/1¾ cups basmati rice

50 g/2 oz. dried rice vermicelli, broken into shorter lengths (optional)

a large handful of fresh mint leaves

50 g/⅓ cup toasted cashew nuts, chopped

SERVES 4

(V)

Put the pickle, onion, garlic and ginger in a food processor and process to make a paste. Heat the oil in a large saucepan. Add the paste and cook, stirring, for 2–3 minutes. Add the carrots and stir-fry for 2–3 minutes. Add the courgettes and stir-fry for about 2 minutes, then turn off the heat.

Bring a large saucepan of water to the boil. Add the rice and cook for 8–10 minutes, until just tender.

Add the rice vermicelli, if using, and cook for another 2–3 minutes, stirring well so that the vermicelli does not stick together and is soft and transparent. Drain well.

Set the saucepan with the vegetables over high heat. Add the rice mixture and stir well until it takes on the golden colour of the curry paste. Stir in the mint and scatter with toasted cashews to serve.

honeyed chicken wings *pictured left*

Here is a fantastic recipe for sweet, sticky, finger-licking chicken wings, served warm – the perfect crowd pleaser on a budget!

16 chicken wings

200 ml/1 cup clear honey

100 ml/²⁄₃ cup sweet chilli sauce

salt and freshly ground black pepper

a bunch of radishes, trimmed, to serve (optional)

SERVES 8

M

Preheat the oven to 200°C (400°F) Gas 6 and grease a roasting tin.

Put the chicken wings into the roasting tin and cook in the preheated oven for 40 minutes, turning them after 20 minutes so they brown evenly all over.

Meanwhile, put the honey and sweet chilli sauce into a small saucepan. Season to taste and bring to the boil. Pour the sauce over the chicken, mix well and leave to cool. Serve with radishes, if using.

pizza with potatoes

Of course, you can put any topping you like on a shop-bought pizza base, but this is fuss-free and needs so few ingredients to make it delicious.

2 x 23–25-cm/10-inch ready-made pizza bases

500 g/1 lb. waxy potatoes, very thinly sliced

2 tablespoons olive oil

4 garlic cloves, crushed

2 sprigs of fresh rosemary, needles pulled off

1 teaspoon salt

MAKES 2

V

Preheat the oven to 220°C (425°F) Gas 7 and put 2 baking trays in to heat up.

Put the potato slices, olive oil, garlic, rosemary needles and salt into a large bowl and toss together to coat.

Spread the potato mixture evenly over both pizzas. Remove the trays from the oven and slide 1 pizza onto each one. Sprinkle with more olive oil and salt if required and bake for 15–20 minutes, or until the potatoes are tender and the pizzas lightly golden and crisp.

warm pasta salad with tuna

Canned fish is one of the most convenient, cost-effective and healthy fast foods to have on hand. It works so well with other simple, fresh Mediterranean flavours, such as lemon and parsley. The inclusion of feta cheese here may seem a little odd, but it really does work. Just a small amount provides an extra tangy, savoury element to this summery dish. Any large, open pasta shape will work.

400 g/14 oz large dried pasta shells, such as lumaconi

65 ml/¼ cup olive oil

2 red onions, finely chopped

2 garlic cloves, finely chopped

1 large red chilli/chile, deseeded and finely chopped

2 tablespoons small salted capers, rinsed

1 tablespoon red wine vinegar

400 g/14 oz canned tuna in oil, well drained

50 g/⅓ cup feta cheese, crumbled

50 g/2 handfuls rocket/arugula

salt and freshly ground black pepper

lemon wedges, to serve

SERVES 4

F

Cook the pasta according to the packet instructions. Drain well and add 1 tablespoon of the olive oil. Transfer to a large bowl.

Heat the remaining oil in a large frying pan/skillet set over high heat. Add the onions, garlic, chilli and capers and cook, stirring, for 2–3 minutes, until the onion has softened. Add the vinegar and cook for a further minute. Add the tuna and use a fork to roughly break up any larger chunks, without mushing the tuna too much.

Add the tuna mixture to the bowl with the pasta. Add the feta and rocket/arugula and gently toss to combine. Season to taste with salt and a generous amount of pepper. Serve warm or cold, as desired, with lemon wedges for squeezing over the top.

spaghetti carbonara

With just four ingredients – eggs, cheese, crème fraîche and black pepper – you can rustle up a rich sauce to create a truly satisfying thrifty supper. The trick here is to add the hot cooked pasta to the beaten egg right before serving to limit its contact with the heat. Returning it to the pan for a moment or two is enough to cook the egg without it scrambling.

200 g/7 oz. dried spaghetti

50 g/3½ tablespoons butter

2 garlic cloves, finely chopped

200 g/7 oz. pancetta or streaky/fatty bacon, cut into small cubes

2 eggs, beaten

75 g/scant ½ cup finely grated Parmesan cheese

a big pinch of fresh parsley, chopped

1 tablespoon crème fraîche (or sour cream)

salt and freshly ground black pepper,

SERVES 2

(M)

First, cook the spaghetti in a saucepan of lightly salted boiling water until it is cooked to your liking. Once the spaghetti is cooked, drain it, reserving 5 mm/¼ inch of the cooking water in the base of the pan, and keep this over low heat.

Meanwhile, melt the butter in a frying pan/skillet over medium heat and fry the garlic until soft. Add the pancetta and fry until crispy and browned. Remove from the heat and keep warm in the pan.

In a large bowl, beat the eggs and then mix in most of the Parmesan cheese, reserving just a little cheese to sprinkle on the top. Add the parsley and crème fraîche and a good crunch of black pepper. Set aside.

Add the drained hot spaghetti to the beaten egg mixture and mix a little, then return the spaghetti and egg mixture to the pan containing the reserved pasta cooking water and stir. You don't want the egg mixture to scramble, but let it mix with the hot pasta water to create a sauce. Stir in the crispy pancetta and garlic mixture.

Serve immediately with the remaining Parmesan cheese sprinkled on top, and a crunch more pepper or a little freshly chopped parsley, as you wish.

spaghetti with chilli & courgettes

This is one of those pasta combinations that works with just about any of your favourite seasonings. You can easily use chilli/hot red pepper flakes instead of fresh chillies/chiles.

400 g/14 oz. spaghetti, or similar pasta

90 ml/⅓ cup olive oil

100 g/¾ cup breadcrumbs

8 small or baby courgettes/zucchini, cut into julienne strips

2 garlic cloves, crushed

2 small red chillies/chiles, deseeded and chopped

grated Parmesan, to serve

SERVES 4

(V)

Cook the spaghetti according to the packet instructions. Drain well and return to the pan to keep warm.

Meanwhile, heat a large frying pan/skillet over medium heat. Add half the olive oil, swirling around to coat the pan, then add the breadcrumbs. Cook for 3–4 minutes, stirring constantly until evenly browned with a nutty aroma. Remove from the pan and wipe the pan clean.

Add the remaining oil to the pan and cook the courgettes for 5 minutes over high heat, turning often, until golden and starting to look crispy. Add the garlic and chillies and cook for 4–5 minutes, stirring often.

Add the cooked pasta and breadcrumbs to the pan, tossing around to combine and serve immediately with grated Parmesan sprinkled over the top.

quick prawn curry

pictured left

Tiger or large/jumbo peeled prawns/ shrimp are ideal for this colourful, citrus-flavoured curry.

200–250 g/7–10 oz. basmati rice

2 tablespoons vegetable oil

1 onion, grated

3 garlic cloves, crushed

5 cm/2 inches fresh ginger, peeled and sliced

1 mild red chilli/chile, chopped

1 teaspoon ground turmeric

2 teaspoons curry powder

1 teaspoon ground coriander

1 teaspoon ground cumin

400 g/1 lb. cooked peeled prawns/shrimp

400-g/14-oz. can chopped tomatoes

juice of 2 limes

freshly chopped coriander/cilantro

SERVES 4

(F)

Cook the rice according to the packet instructions.

Meanwhile, heat the oil in a large pan, add the onion, garlic, ginger and chilli and cook for 5 minutes over medium heat. Add the turmeric, curry powder, ground coriander and cumin and mix well. Add the prawns/shrimp and cook for 3 minutes.

Pour in the tomatoes and lime juice, season with salt and pepper and bring to the boil. Reduce the heat and simmer for 5 minutes. Garnish with freshly chopped coriander and serve with the cooked rice.

Variation: For a vegetarian option, replace the prawns with 200 g/8 oz. halved button mushrooms and 200 g/8 oz. frozen peas.

white spaghetti

This is one of those dishes that saves your life when you get home tired and hungry. Always keep some anchovies, olive oil and spaghetti in the cupboard to make this at short notice.

150 g/6 oz. dried pasta, such as spaghetti

6 tablespoons/⅓ cup olive oil

4 garlic cloves, halved

6 anchovy fillets in oil, drained

salt and freshly ground black pepper

SERVES 2

(V)

Bring a large saucepan of water to the boil. Add a good pinch of salt, then the pasta, and cook until al dente, or according to the manufacturer's instructions.

Put the olive oil and garlic in a small saucepan and heat very gently over low heat for 4–5 minutes until the garlic is pale golden but not browned. Remove and discard the garlic.

Add the anchovies and 100 ml/⅓ cup water to the pan and simmer rapidly, whisking with the fork until the anchovies have almost dissolved into the mixture. Add plenty of pepper and a tiny pinch of salt.

Drain the pasta and return it to the warm pan. Add the anchovy mixture and toss well to mix. Transfer to bowls and serve.

lamb in pita bread

To make this tasty dinner even more thrifty, you could swap the lamb for beef or even turkey – use whatever you have in the freezer or whatever is on offer at the supermarket.

2 teaspoons coriander seeds

1 teaspoon cumin seeds

2 tablespoons olive oil

1 onion, finely chopped

2 garlic cloves, crushed

1 teaspoon ground cinnamon

¼–½ teaspoon cayenne pepper

300 g/10 oz. minced/ground lamb

a pinch of salt

2 tablespoons chopped fresh coriander/cilantro

4 pita breads

a few salad leaves/greens

natural/plain yoghurt

1 tablespoon sesame seeds, toasted in a dry frying pan/skillet

SERVES 4

(M)

Put the coriander and cumin seeds into a small frying pan/skillet without oil and fry until they start to brown and release their aroma. Leave to cool slightly, then grind to powder with a pestle and mortar.

Heat the oil in a frying pan/skillet, add the onion, garlic and ground spices and fry gently for 5 minutes until softened but not golden. Increase the heat, add the lamb and the pinch of salt and stir-fry for 5–8 minutes until well browned. Stir in the fresh coriander.

Meanwhile, lightly toast the pita breads and cut a long slit in the side of each one. Carefully fill with a few salad leaves, add the lamb mixture, a spoonful of yoghurt and sprinkle with sesame seeds. Serve hot.

smoked seafood tagliatelle pictured on front cover

The canned mussels give an instant depth of flavour, along with the oil from the can which they have infused with their smokiness. Using canned seafood is an easy way to make a thrifty meal seem much more luxurious.

85-g/3-oz. can smoked mussels in oil

2 garlic cloves, sliced

400-g/14-oz can cherry tomatoes

a pinch of sugar

a very small pinch of chilli/hot red pepper flakes

½ teaspoon ground cinnamon

250 g/9 oz. dried tagliatelle or spaghetti

2 x 110-g/4-oz. cans squid in oil, drained

a few sprigs of fresh flat-leaf parsley or coriander/cilantro, chopped

salt and freshly ground black pepper

SERVES 4

(F)

Pour the oil from the can of mussels into a pan and gently warm the sliced garlic for a couple of minutes. Partly open the can of cherry tomatoes, drain off about half the juice (save the drained juice for another recipe) and tip the remaining tomatoes and juice into the pan. Add the sugar, chilli and cinnamon. Leave the pan on a low simmer with the lid off to reduce and cook out the acidity of the tomatoes.

While the sauce is simmering, cook the tagliatelle in a pan of salted boiling water following the packet instructions for al dente – about 8 minutes.

Just before the pasta is cooked, add the smoked mussels and the squid to the pan of sauce (no need to add the oil from the squid) and fold it all together, seasoning with freshly ground black pepper and a pinch of sea salt flakes.

Finally, using a pair of tongs, pull the pasta from the pot and place into the pan with the sauce, lift it a couple of times to incorporate, then leave on the heat for another minute to help the pasta absorb all those delicious flavours. Serve with a scattering of parsley or coriander over the top; sometimes I give it a drizzle of olive oil too.

vegetable noodle stir-fry

When making this dish, prepare the ingredients in advance, so the stir-fry can be quickly put together. You can vary the vegetables but always use the onion, garlic, ginger and chilli/chile where possible.

4 tablespoons/¼ cup vegetable/safflower oil

1 garlic clove, crushed

5 cm/2 inches fresh ginger, peeled and finely chopped

1 onion, thinly sliced

1 chilli/chile, finely chopped

125 g/4 oz. egg noodles

2 pak-choi/bok choy, roughly chopped

1 leek, cut into strips

75 g/1½ cups beansprouts, trimmed

75 g/1¼ cups mushrooms, sliced

3 tablespoons soy sauce

juice of 1 lime

a bunch of fresh coriander/cilantro, chopped

SERVES 4

Heat the oil in a large frying pan/skillet. Add the garlic, ginger, onion and chilli and cook over medium heat, stirring constantly.

Bring a large saucepan of water to the boil. Add the noodles and cook according to the manufacturer's instructions. Drain thoroughly.

Add the pak-choi, leek, beansprouts and mushrooms to the frying pan/skillet and stir-fry for 2–3 minutes.

Add the soy sauce, lime juice and noodles and use 2 spoons to mix the vegetables and noodles together. Top with the chopped coriander and serve immediately.

chicken & lemon skewers

These yoghurt-crusted chicken skewers makes ideal finger food so are perfect for feeding a crowd on a budget, and are super quick to prepare and cook too. The yoghurt tenderizes the chicken and helps the lemon soak into the meat.

500 g/1 lb. skinless, boneless chicken breasts

marinade

250 g/1 cup plain yoghurt

2 tablespoons extra virgin olive oil

2 garlic cloves, crushed

grated zest and freshly squeezed

juice of 1 unwaxed lemon

1–2 teaspoons chilli/chili powder

1 tablespoon chopped fresh coriander/cilantro

salt and freshly ground black pepper

12 bamboo skewers, soaked in cold water for 30 minutes

SERVES 4

Cut the chicken lengthways into 2-mm/⅛-inch strips and put in a shallow ceramic dish.

Put all the marinade ingredients in a bowl, stir well, and pour over the chicken. Turn to coat, cover and let marinate in the refrigerator overnight.

The next day, thread the chicken onto the soaked bamboo skewers, zig-zagging the meat back and forth as you go.

Cook on a preheated barbecue or under a hot grill/broiler for 3–4 minutes on each side until charred and tender. Let cool slightly before serving.

beefburgers/hamburgers

Burgers are fantastically versatile, so build yours just as you like, with or without the suggested garnishes.

600 g/1 lb. 4 oz. minced/ground beef

1 garlic clove, crushed

1 shallot, finely diced

a bunch of fresh parsley, chopped

1 tablespoon olive oil

1 teaspoon Worcestershire sauce

4 rashers/slices of (streaky) bacon

4 ciabatta rolls

4 tablespoons/¼ cup mayonnaise

4 slices of beef tomato

100 g/1 cup Cheddar, grated

1 avocado, sliced

shredded iceberg lettuce

salt and freshly ground black pepper

MAKES 4

(M)

Preheat the grill/broiler.

Put the beef, garlic, shallot, parsley and Worcestershire sauce in a large bowl, season with salt and pepper and mix well with your hands. Divide the mixture into 4 and shape into burgers.

Heat some oil in a large frying pan/skillet and cook the patties for 2 minutes on each side for rare, 3 minutes for medium-rare and 4 minutes for well done.

Meanwhile, grill/broil the bacon until crisp. Cut the ciabatta rolls in half and grill/broil the insides. Spread the grilled sides with mayonnaise. Put a slice of tomato on the grilled base and a burger on top, followed by a handful of cheese, a bacon rasher, a slice or two of avocado and some lettuce. Sandwich together with the remaining bread and serve with ketchup and mustard.

caldo verde

This rustic Portuguese soup is substantial enough to serve as a meal in its own right, using only a small list of ingredients, making it budget-friendly too. Serve with a few slices of chorizo on the top and some fresh bread on the side.

1 tablespoon extra virgin olive oil, plus extra for serving

1 onion, chopped

1 garlic clove, chopped

400 g/14 oz. floury potatoes, peeled and chopped

600 ml/2½ cups chicken or vegetable stock

150 g/3 cups kale

1 cooking chorizo, finely sliced (optional)

salt and freshly ground black pepper

rustic bread, to serve

SERVES 4

(M)

Heat the olive oil in a large saucepan. Gently fry the onion and garlic, stirring often so as to prevent them from burning, for 2 minutes, until the onion and garlic have softened.

Add the potatoes and stock and season with salt and freshly ground black pepper. Bring to the boil, reduce the heat, cover and simmer for 15 minutes.

Tear the leaves off the kale, discarding the tough stalks. Roll up the leaves tightly and slice them as thinly as possible into shreds. Alternatively, chop the kale into thick ribbons.

Remove the simmered soup from the heat and roughly mash the softened potatoes into the soup, leaving some chunks. Return the soup to the hob/stovetop, bring to the boil and add the kale. Simmer for 2–3 minutes until the kale is just tender.

Meanwhile, fry the chorizo slices (if using) in a frying pan/skillet until cooked through and lightly browned.

Serve each portion of soup with a few chorizo slices (if using) on top, some freshly ground black pepper and a splash of extra virgin olive oil.

quick vegetable curry

This is a cheat's curry using a ready-made curry paste, which cuts down on the ingredients needed. Serve with basmati rice.

3 tablespoons sunflower oil

1 onion, sliced

2 garlic cloves, chopped

3 cm/1 inch fresh ginger, peeled and grated

1 tablespoon hot red curry paste

1 teaspoon ground cinnamon

500 g/1 lb. baking potatoes, cubed

400 g/14 oz. canned chopped tomatoes

300 ml/1¼ cups vegetable stock

1 tablespoon tomato purée/paste

200 g/8 oz. button mushrooms

200 g/8 oz. frozen peas

25 g/⅓ cup finely ground almonds

2 tablespoons chopped fresh coriander/cilantro

salt and freshly ground black pepper

SERVES 4

Heat the oil in a saucepan and fry the onion, garlic, ginger, curry paste and cinnamon for 5 minutes. Add the potatoes, tomatoes, stock, tomato purée, salt and pepper. Bring to the boil, cover and simmer gently for 20 minutes.

Halve the mushrooms and add them to the pan with the peas, ground almonds and coriander and cook for a further 10 minutes. Taste and adjust the seasoning with salt and pepper, then serve.

cauliflower potato curry

This quickly-made, dry vegetable curry is gutsy, piquant and fragrant. Serve it with chapatis or steamed basmati rice for a vegan meal; ideal for a mid-week supper.

300 g/10½ oz. waxy potatoes

1 cauliflower, cut into florets

1½ tablespoons vegetable or sunflower oil

1 onion, finely chopped

2-cm/¾-inch piece of fresh ginger, peeled and finely chopped

1 garlic clove, chopped

1 teaspoon fennel seeds

1 teaspoon mustard seeds

2 teaspoons ground cumin

1 teaspoon ground turmeric

½ teaspoon chilli/chili powder

2 tablespoons tomato purée/paste

150 ml/scant ⅔ cup hot water

1 teaspoon sugar

salt

freshly chopped coriander/cilantro, to garnish

SERVES 4

(V)

Cook the potatoes in boiling, salted water until tender; drain and quarter. In a separate pan, par-boil the cauliflower in boiling, salted water for 5 minutes until just tender; drain.

Heat the oil in a large, heavy-based frying pan/skillet over medium heat. Fry the onion, stirring often, for 5 minutes, until softened. Add the ginger, garlic, fennel seeds and mustard seeds and fry, stirring, for 2 minutes until fragrant.

Mix the cumin, turmeric and chilli powder with a tablespoon of cold water to make a spice paste. Add the spice paste to the onion mixture and cook, stirring, for 1 minute. Add the potato quarters and cauliflower, mixing in well.

Mix the tomato purée into the hot water and add to the potato mixture. Season with salt and add the sugar. Mix well. Bring to the boil, cover and cook for 5 minutes, stirring every now and then. Garnish with coriander and serve.

4

snacks & sides

carrot, orange & cumin dip

This is an aromatic, tangy dip perfect to serve with vegetable crudités or savoury wafers. You barely need any ingredients so the chances are that you can rustle it up even if your fridge and kitchen cupboards are looking a little bare.

500 g/1 lb. carrots, chopped

2 tablespoons olive oil

1 small onion, finely chopped

1 garlic clove, chopped

1 teaspoon ground cumin

75 ml/⅓ cup orange juice

salt and freshly ground black pepper

crackers, to serve

SERVES 4–6

V

Steam the carrots for 15–20 minutes, or until tender.

Meanwhile, heat the olive oil in a frying pan/skillet and gently fry the onion, garlic and cumin for 5 minutes, or until softened.

Transfer to a food processor, add the carrots, orange juice and seasoning and blend until smooth. Season to taste and leave to cool.

Serve at room temperature with crackers. Store in a screw-top jar in the fridge for up to 2 days.

bagna cauda

Made from storecupboard essentials, this warm anchovy butter is best served with an assortment of fresh summer vegetables – just let everyone help themselves.

50 g/4 tablespoons unsalted butter

4 large garlic cloves, crushed

50 g/2 oz. anchovy fillets in oil, drained and chopped

200 ml/¾ cup olive oil

SERVES 4–6

(F)

Heat the butter and garlic together in a small saucepan and cook very gently for 4–5 minutes, or until softened but not browned.

Add the anchovies, stir well, then pour in the olive oil. Cook gently for 10 minutes, stirring every now and then until the sauce has softened and is almost creamy. Serve warm.

pesto

This is a homemade version of this storecupboard staple that is used by cooks throughout the world to serve with pasta or grilled fish, or be stirred into vegetable soup. Once made, cover the surface with a little extra olive oil, seal in a container and refrigerate for up to 5 days.

50 g/2 handfuls fresh basil leaves	2 tablespoons grated Parmesan
1 garlic clove, crushed	400 g/14 oz. pasta
2 tablespoons pine nuts	black pepper
a pinch of salt	SERVES 4
6–8 tablespoons/¼–⅓ cup olive oil	V

Put the basil, garlic, pine nuts and salt in a mortar and pound to form a fairly smooth paste. Add the olive oil slowly until you reach a texture that is soft but not runny. Add the Parmesan and pepper to taste.

Cook the pasta according to the packet instructions. Drain well, add the pesto and stir through before serving.

Alternatively, cover the surface with a little olive oil and refrigerate for up to 3 days.

Tip: You can make this sauce in a food processor, but do not over-process otherwise the sauce will be too smooth.

tapenade

Using niçoise olives will give the finished sauce a truly authentic flavour. It is preferable to buy whole olives and pit them yourself – to do this simply press down firmly on the olives using a thumb and the flesh will split to reveal the stone, which is then discarded.

125 g/4 oz. niçoise olives	4 tablespoons/¼ cup olive oil
2 canned anchovy fillets in oil, drained	a squeeze of lemon juice
2 garlic cloves, crushed	400 g/14 oz. pasta
2 tablespoons capers in brine, drained and rinsed	black pepper
1 teaspoon Dijon mustard	SERVES 4
	F

Put the olives, anchovies, garlic, capers and mustard in a mortar (or food processor) and pound to form a fairly smooth paste. Gradually blend in the olive oil and add lemon juice and pepper to taste.

Cook the pasta according to the packet instructions. Drain well, add the tapenade and stir through before serving.

Alternatively, transfer to a dish, cover and refrigerate for up to 5 days.

hummus

This tasty, nutty-flavoured Middle Eastern dip is so easy to make at home and is the perfect thrifty snack made from canned chickpeas/garbanzo beans. Serve it with pita bread, falafel or vegetable crudités for a light meal.

125 g/¾ cup dried chickpeas/ garbanzo beans

1 teaspoon bicarbonate of soda/baking soda

2 garlic cloves, crushed to a paste

4 tablespoons tahini

freshly squeezed juice of 1 lemon

salt

to garnish

olive oil

paprika or sumac

finely chopped fresh parsley

SERVES 6

(V)

Soak the chickpeas overnight in plenty of cold water with the bicarbonate of soda.

Next day, drain and rinse. Place in a large pan, add enough fresh cold water to cover well and bring to the boil. Reduce the heat and simmer for 50–60 minutes until tender, skimming off any scum. Season the chickpeas with salt, then drain, reserving the cooking water and setting aside 1 tablespoon of the cooked chickpeas for the garnish.

In a food processor, blend together the cooked chickpeas, garlic, tahini and lemon juice. Gradually add the cooking liquid until the mixture becomes a smooth paste. Season with salt.

Transfer the hummus to a serving bowl. To serve, make a shallow hollow in the centre using the back of a spoon. Pour in a little olive oil, top with the reserved whole chickpeas and sprinkle with paprika and parsley.

fettunta pictured left

The original 'garlic bread', this Italian dish is traditionally made using the new season's olive oil, although any good-quality extra virgin olive oil can be used. In classic Italian fashion, simple ingredients combine to great effect. The name translates literally as 'oily slice', but it is far more delicious than this name may suggest. Although quick and simple to make, it is so tasty.

4 thick slices of rustic bread

1 garlic clove, peeled

4 tablespoons extra virgin olive oil

salt (optional)

a griddle pan

MAKES 4 SLICES

V

Preheat a griddle pan until hot.

Griddle the bread for 2–3 minutes on each side until golden-brown and nicely striped. If you don't have a griddle pan, preheat a grill/broiler and toast until golden brown on each side.

Immediately rub one side of each slice with the garlic clove. Pour a tablespoon of olive oil over each slice. Add a pinch of salt, if using, and serve at once.

tzatziki

This delicate, refreshing and garlicky Greek dip is a classic. Serve with kebabs/kabobs or with pita bread or crudités for a snack.

½ cucumber

1 garlic clove, crushed

250 g/1 cup Greek yoghurt

1 tablespoon chopped fresh mint leaves

1 tablespoon olive oil

1 teaspoon white wine vinegar

salt

SERVES 8

V

Peel the cucumber and grate it. Sprinkle with salt and set aside for 15 minutes to draw out the moisture. Drain and pat dry with paper towels.

Mix the grated cucumber, garlic, yoghurt, chopped mint, olive oil and vinegar together in a medium bowl. Cover and chill until ready to serve.

tomatoey green beans with onion & fennel seeds

Spice up your customary boiled green beans with fragrant fennel seeds, onions and a dash of tomato purée/paste.

500 g/1 lb. green beans, trimmed

4 tablespoons/¼ cup olive oil

1 onion, thinly sliced

1 teaspoon fennel seeds, lightly crushed

1 tablespoon tomato purée/ paste

salt and freshly ground black pepper

SERVES 4

[V]

Bring a saucepan of salted water to the boil and add the beans. Boil for about 6 minutes until tender but still slightly crisp.

Meanwhile, heat the olive oil in a frying pan/skillet and cook the onion for about 5 minutes until just beginning to colour and soften.

Drain the beans and set aside.

Add the crushed fennel seeds to the onion with plenty of salt and pepper. Mix the tomato purée/paste with 100 ml/⅓ cup warm water and add to the onion mixture. Bring to the boil and stir in the beans, tossing well to coat with the sauce. Taste and season again. Cover and simmer gently for 5 minutes, then serve.

sautéed greens pictured left

This method of cooking sprouts and cabbage ensures that they remain crisp and tasty. A great match with pork.

400 g/14 oz. Brussels sprouts

1 tablespoon olive oil

1 tablespoon butter

1 teaspoon caraway seeds

¼ green cabbage, thinly sliced

½ iceberg lettuce, cut into 1-cm/½-inch slices

juice of ½ lemon

½ teaspoon salt

SERVES 4–6

(V)

Separate as many leaves as you can from the sprouts and then finely slice any remaining leaves that are too tight to separate. Set aside.

Heat a large frying pan/skillet or wok. Add the oil and butter and heat to medium. Add the caraway seeds and sizzle for about 30 seconds. Add the Brussels sprouts and cabbage and stir fry for about 4 minutes, or until wilted. Add the lettuce, stir-fry for a further minute, then quickly transfer to a serving dish to stop the cooking.

Pour over the lemon juice and sprinkle with the salt. Toss and serve.

cauliflower with anchovies

Cauliflowers are not just for cauliflower cheese. Try this lighter approach if you fancy a change.

1 dried bay leaf

2 cauliflowers, about 600 g/1¼ lbs., separated into florets

3–5 tablespoons olive oil

3 long, thin inner celery sticks, finely chopped, plus a handful of leaves, chopped

6 canned anchovy fillets in oil, chopped

3–4 garlic cloves, finely chopped

juice of ½ lemon

Tabasco sauce (optional)

salt and freshly ground black pepper

SERVES 4

(F)

Bring a large saucepan of water to the boil with the bay leaf. Add a generous amount of salt, then the cauliflower. Cook for 2–3 minutes just to blanch. Drain and set aside.

Heat 3 tablespoons of the oil in a large frying pan/skillet. Add the celery stalks and cook for 1 minute. Add the cauliflower and a good pinch of salt and cook for 2–3 minutes over medium-high heat, without stirring.

Add the remaining oil if it needs it (this dish can be slightly oily), then the anchovies, and cook for 2–3 minutes more. Add the garlic, stir well and cook for 30 seconds – do not let the garlic burn. Remove from the heat and stir in the celery leaves. Add the lemon juice and salt and pepper to taste. Add a few drops of Tabasco if you like. Serve hot or at room temperature.

sautéed potatoes with bacon & garlic

This is definitely a dish for garlic-lovers! Frying the potatoes with garlic instead of onion adds a rich umami tastiness to this classic potato dish. Serve it with poached or fried eggs for a substantial breakfast or a light lunch.

500 g/17½ oz. waxy potatoes

12 garlic cloves

100 g/3½ oz. thick-cut bacon or pancetta, cut into short strips

1 tablespoon olive oil

salt and freshly ground black pepper

2 tablespoons freshly chopped parsley

SERVES 4

(M)

Cook the potatoes in boiling, salted water until tender. Drain and cut into 5-mm/¼-inch-thick slices.

Blanch the garlic cloves in a separate small pan of boiling water for 5 minutes, until tender. Drain and then peel.

Fry the bacon in a heavy-based frying pan/skillet over medium heat for 2–3 minutes. Add the olive oil, heat through and then add the potato slices. Fry, stirring often, for 5–7 minutes until the potato slices are golden brown on both sides.

Add the peeled garlic cloves and fry for 2–3 minutes until lightly golden. Season with salt and freshly ground black pepper. Sprinkle with the parsley and serve at once.

herbed crushed potatoes

Crushing potatoes is a very easy way of preparing them, as no peeling is required! The roughly crushed potatoes soak up the flavours of the dressing, while the use of lemon zest and herbs give a real lift to the dish. This is a great way of using up any leftover herbs that you have lying around.

500 g/17½ oz. even-sized waxy potatoes

2 tablespoons extra virgin olive oil

grated zest of ½ lemon

1 teaspoon freshly squeezed lemon juice

2 tablespoons freshly chopped chives

2 tablespoons freshly chopped mint leaves

3 tablespoons finely chopped parsley

salt and freshly ground black pepper

SERVES 4

(V)

Cook the potatoes in boiling, salted water until tender, then drain.

Return the potatoes to the pan. Use a masher to roughly crush them, making sure not to totally mash them.

Add the olive oil, lemon zest and juice and season with salt and freshly ground black pepper, mixing well. Add the chives, mint and parsley and mix in.

Serve warm or at room temperature.

potato cheese scones

Floury potatoes give a delightfully light texture to these traditional savoury scones, best eaten hot from the pan, topped with cold butter. Serve for breakfast or a tea-time treat.

450 g/15¾ oz. floury potatoes, peeled and chopped

25 g/1½ tablespoons butter

50 g/½ cup grated Cheddar cheese

25 g/⅓ cup grated Parmesan cheese

75 g/½ cup self-raising/rising flour, plus extra for dusting

salt and freshly ground black pepper

butter, to serve

MAKES 24 SCONES

V

Cook the potatoes in boiling, salted water until tender; drain and transfer to a bowl. Add the butter, Cheddar and Parmesan and mash together well.

Stir in the flour to form a soft dough. Season with salt and freshly ground black pepper.

On a lightly floured surface, pat out the dough to 1 cm/ ½ inch thickness. Cut into 24 triangles.

Preheat a large, heavy-based frying pan/skillet or griddle/grill pan until very hot. Add the potato triangles, cooking them in two batches. Fry the potato scones for 3 minutes on each side, until browned on both sides. Serve at once with butter.

Mexican red rice

Rice is the perfect thrifty storecupboard staple and is great for stretching out a meal to make it go further. It can be quite bland though, so this recipe takes it up a notch. Tomatoes give a delicate sweetness to the rice, with a touch of heat from the chilli/chile. Serve as a tasty side dish with grilled chicken or steak and a tomato salsa.

200 g/½ lb. tomatoes

1 tablespoon vegetable oil

½ onion, peeled and finely chopped

1 garlic clove, peeled and sliced

1 red chilli/chile, chopped

200 g/1 cup long-grain rice, rinsed

250 ml/1 cup chicken or vegetable stock

salt, to taste

50 g/½ cup frozen peas (optional)

SERVES 4

(V) or (M)

Begin by scalding the tomatoes. Pour boiling water over the ripe tomatoes in a heatproof bowl. Set aside for 1 minute, then drain and carefully peel off the skin using a sharp knife. Roughly chop, reserving any juices, and set aside.

Heat the oil in a heavy bottomed saucepan or pot set over medium heat. Add the onion and garlic and fry until softened. Add the chilli and fry for another minute, then add the chopped tomatoes with their juices. Increase the heat, stir well, and cook until the tomatoes have broken down and form a thick paste.

Mix in the rice and pour over the stock. Season with salt, bring the mixture to the boil and add the frozen peas, if using. Cover, reduce the heat and cook for 10–15 minutes until the stock has been absorbed and the rice is cooked through.

5

sweet treats

baked lemon pudding

pictured left

This is an old family favourite and perfect for when lemons are in abundance and inexpensive at your local food store or market.

50 g/3 tablespoons unsalted butter

285 g/2½ cups caster sugar

3 eggs, separated

3 tablespoons self-raising/rising flour

375 ml/1½ cups whole milk

65 ml/¼ cup lemon juice

1 tablespoon icing/confectioners' sugar

a medium baking dish

SERVES 6

V

Preheat the oven to 180°C (350°F) Gas 4.

Put the butter and sugar in a food processor and process for 10 seconds, until smooth. Add the egg yolks one at a time to the mixture and process for a few seconds after each addition. Add the flour and process until smooth. With the motor running pour in the milk in a slow and steady stream, scraping down the bowl of the food processer with a spatula so all the mixture is incorporated and lump free. Transfer the mixture to a large bowl.

Using an electric whisk, beat the egg whites until firm, then fold them into the batter in two batches using a large metal spoon. Quickly stir in the lemon juice.

Spoon the mixture into the baking dish and bake in the preheated oven for 25 minutes, or until golden on top. Leave to rest for 10 minutes before dusting with icing sugar to serve.

strawberries with black pepper

Strawberries and black pepper are surprisingly good partners. The orange flower water adds a lovely perfumed quality to the strawberries, but can be omitted.

500 g/1 lb. strawberries

1 tablespoon orange flower water (optional)

1 tablespoon caster/superfine sugar

2 teaspoons cracked black pepper

SERVES 4

V

Hull the strawberries and cut in half. Sprinkle with the orange flower water, if using, and with the sugar and black pepper. Chill for 15 minutes.

Note: Strawberries should be washed and dried before hulling, not after, otherwise they fill up with water.

iced summer berries with hot white chocolate sauce

This is the ultimate in simple puddings – if you have these ingredients in your fridge, freezer and storecupboard, you will never be caught out by unexpected guests. The secret is to make sure that the summer fruits are just frozen before pouring over the hot white chocolate sauce.

175 g/6 oz. white chocolate, chopped

150 ml/⅔ cup single/whipping cream

1 teaspoon lavender honey

450 g/1 lb. frozen mixed summer berries (such as blueberries, strawberries, raspberries, blackberries and redcurrants)

SERVES 4

(V)

Remove the summer berries from the freezer 10 minutes before you want to serve them.

Put the white chocolate, cream and honey in a heatproof bowl and set over a pan of simmering water. Do not let the base of the bowl touch the water. Stir continuously with a rubber or wooden spatula, until the chocolate has melted and you have a smooth sauce. Alternatively, you can melt the chocolate with the cream and honey in the microwave. Be careful because white chocolate scorches easily, so don't overcook it.

Arrange the semi-frozen berries on individual serving plates, then pour the hot white chocolate sauce all over the berries so that the heat of the sauce begins to melt and soften them. Serve immediately.

sticky fried bananas on toast pictured left

One mouthful of these buttery, sticky, gooey, tangy bananas will transport you to another world – just be careful about putting too much in your mouth in one go because those bananas are HOT when they first come out of the pan! Challah, the delicious, dense Jewish bread, makes the perfect base, but any good-quality white bread will be divine.

50 g/4 tablespoons unsalted butter, plus extra for spreading

3 perfectly ripe bananas, sliced

2 tablespoons brown sugar

1 tablespoon brandy

½ lime

2 thick slices of challah or white bread

vanilla ice cream, to serve

SERVES 2

(V)

Melt the butter in a non-stick pan until sizzling, then add the bananas and fry for about 2 minutes. Turn them over, sprinkle with the brown sugar and continue cooking for a further 2–3 minutes, gently nudging the bananas around the pan, but take care not to break them up.

Add the brandy and cook for 1 minute more until the bananas are soft and tender, letting the juices bubble. Remove the pan from the heat, squeeze over the lime juice and jiggle the bananas to mix.

Meanwhile, lightly toast the bread on both sides. Add the bananas and top with a generous scoop of vanilla ice cream. Serve immediately.

banana fritters

Fruit fritters are delicious and so simple to make. They take no time at all to prepare so even if you haven't planned to have dessert, you can probably rustle this up without too much bother.

2 large bananas

cinnamon ice cream, to serve (optional)

ginger batter

40 g/⅓ cup plain/all-purpose flour

a pinch of salt

1 egg, separated

75 ml/⅓ cup ginger beer or sparkling water

1 tablespoon sunflower/safflower oil, plus extra for deep-frying

SERVES 4

(V)

Preheat the oven to a very low setting.

Peel the bananas, cut into 4 chunks, then cut the chunks in half lengthways.

To make the batter, sift the flour and salt into a bowl, beat in the egg yolk, ginger beer or sparkling water and oil to form a smooth batter. Whisk the egg white in a separate bowl until soft peaks form, then fold into the batter.

Heat 5 cm/2 inches sunflower/safflower oil in deep saucepan until it reaches 180°C (350°F) or until a cube of bread turns golden brown in 30 seconds.

Dip the banana chunks into the batter and deep-fry in batches of 3–4 for about 1 minute until the batter is crisp and golden. Drain on kitchen paper and keep them warm in a moderate oven while you cook the remainder. Serve with a scoop of cinnamon ice cream, if you like.

zabaglione

There is nothing quite as sensual as warm zabaglione served straight from the pan. The secret is not to let the mixture get too hot, but still hot enough to cook and thicken the egg yolks. The proportions are easy to remember: one egg yolk to one tablespoon sugar to one tablespoon Marsala, serves one person. It must be made at the last moment, but it doesn't take long and is well worth the effort. A delicious dessert from just a couple of simple ingredients.

2 large egg yolks

2 tablespoons sweet Marsala wine

2 tablespoons caster/superfine sugar

sponge fingers/ladyfingers, for dipping

SERVES 2

(V)

Put the egg yolks, Marsala and sugar in a medium heatproof bowl (preferably copper or stainless steel) and beat with an electric whisk or a balloon whisk until well blended.

Set the bowl over a saucepan of gently simmering water but do not let the bowl touch the water. Do not let the water boil. Whisk the mixture until it is glossy, pale, light and fluffy and holds a trail when dropped from the whisk. This should take about 5 minutes.

Serve immediately in warmed cocktail glasses with sponge fingers/ladyfingers for dipping.

cheat's cherry brûlée

Real crème brûlée is creamy, indulgent and a bit fiddly to make. This is the cheat's alternative. Don't be put off by needing fancy crème fraîche and fromage frais – they are now both easy to find in your local supermarket, and you can use up any leftovers with freshly chopped fruit for breakfast.

300 g/10 oz. fresh, ripe cherries, stoned

100 ml/⅓ cup crème fraîche/ light cream

100 ml/⅓ cup fromage frais/ cream cheese

1 teaspoon vanilla extract

4 tablespoons/¼ cup demerara/ brown sugar

4 ramekins, 150 ml/5 oz. each

SERVES 4

(V)

Preheat the grill/broiler.

Put the cherries in a saucepan with 100 ml/½ cup water. Cook over high heat until simmering, then lower the heat and simmer gently until the fruit is slightly softened, 5–7 minutes. Remove the pan from the heat.

Put the crème fraîche, fromage frais and vanilla extract in a bowl and mix well.

Divide the cherries between the 4 ramekins. Spoon the cream mixture over the cherries, then top each serving with 1 tablespoon of the demerara sugar.

Put the ramekins under the grill/broiler until the sugar melts and begins to caramelize. Remove from the heat and serve immediately.

Note: Fresh cherries can sometimes be quite pricey to buy, so feel free to use frozen cherries as a more budget-friendly alternative.

nutty chocolate & marshmallow toast

Sinfully sweet and sticky, this toast is the ultimate in instant comfort food. It's lacking sophistication by anyone's standards – but it makes a luscious treat when you're feeling blue and need a no-effort pick-me-up.

2 thick slices of white bread

2 tablespoons single/light cream

15 g/½ oz. plain/semisweet chocolate, grated or shaved, or plain chocolate chips

15 g/handful shelled pecan nuts

25 g/handful mini-marshmallows

SERVES 2

(V)

Preheat the grill/broiler.

Toast the bread on one side under the grill/broiler, then flip over. Pour the cream over the untoasted side, sprinkle with the grated or shaved chocolate, nuts and marshmallows and grill until golden and bubbling. Eat with caution: the topping will be hot!

Note: You can use any type of white bread – a classic square white loaf, a white bloomer or several slices of white baguette cut diagonally.

strawberry sundaes

pictured left

Layers of fresh strawberry sauce and crushed amaretti biscuits with creamy vanilla yoghurt custard make a delicious dessert. A little goes a long way, so you could make smaller portions to feed more people.

275 g/9 oz. very ripe strawberries, hulled

200 ml/¾ cup natural/ Greek yoghurt

250 ml/1 cup ready- made custard/vanilla yoghurt

½ teaspoon vanilla extract (optional)

6 amaretti biscuits, roughly broken

SERVES 2–4

V

Set aside 4 strawberries to decorate. Purée the remaining fruit by pressing it through a sieve. Set aside.

Mix together the yoghurt, custard and vanilla extract, if using, in a bowl.

Spoon a layer of the yoghurt mixture into two tall glasses. Top with a layer of strawberry purée and amaretti biscuits. Repeat with another layer of yoghurt mixture, the remaining purée and amaretti. Top with a final layer of yoghurt mixture.

Slice the reserved strawberries and use to decorate the sundaes.

melon with ginger syrup

Melon and ginger are a classic combination of flavours and this simple version is perfect for a warm summer's day. You can use any type of melon, but cantaloupe works particularly well.

75 g/4 tablespoons caster/superfine sugar

2.5 cm/1 inch fresh ginger, peeled and finely chopped

juice of ½ large lemon

1 large, ripe melon

SERVES 4–6

V

Put the sugar and 150 ml/⅔ cup water into a small saucepan and heat gently to dissolve the sugar. Bring to the boil, add the ginger and lemon juice and simmer gently for 3 minutes. Remove from the heat and leave to cool.

Cut the melon into wedges, scoop out the seeds and serve drizzled with ginger syrup.

pan plum crumble

This comforting crumble is cooked under the grill/broiler and you can even serve it at the table straight out of the frying pan/skillet – it doesn't get any more casual than that! The crumble is finished under the grill/broiler so use a frying pan/skillet with a heatproof handle.

185 ml/¾ cup orange juice

2 tablespoons caster/superfine sugar

6 ripe plums, halved and stoned

100 g/¾ cup self-raising/rising flour

60 g/⅓ cup soft/packed brown sugar

60 g/½ cup porridge/rolled oats

50 g/4 tablespoons unsalted butter, chilled and cubed

SERVES 4–6

(V)

Put the orange juice and caster sugar in a small frying pan/skillet over high heat. Bring the mixture to the boil, then reduce the heat to medium. Add the plums, cut-side down, and cook for 5 minutes. Turn the plums over and cook for a further 5 minutes, until they have softened yet still retain their shape and the liquid has almost evaporated. Remove the pan from the heat and set aside.

Preheat the grill/broiler to medium.

Put the flour, brown sugar and oats in a bowl and mix just to combine. Add the butter and use your fingertips to rub it into the dry ingredients.

Sprinkle the mixture evenly over the plums and slide the frying pan/skillet under the grill/broiler for 2–3 minutes, until the crumble is golden. Serve warm.

pan-fried Caribbean bananas

This dessert is superb topped with a dollop of crème fraîche or fromage frais/sour cream, and perhaps a sprinkling of pumpkin seeds. It's super-quick, and quite healthy, so you don't need to feel guilty about having dessert after a big meal!

1 tablespoon margarine

1 tablespoon runny honey

2 bananas, cut into 1-cm/
½-inch slices

25 g/2 tablespoons sultanas/
golden raisins

1 tablespoon dark rum
(optional)

juice of 1 small orange

SERVES 2

(V)

Melt the margarine and honey in a non-stick frying pan/skillet over high heat. Add the bananas and fry for 2–3 minutes until they are golden and softened.

Quickly stir in the sultanas, rum, if using, and orange juice. Bubble for about 30 seconds, then spoon into bowls and serve immediately.

index

recipe credits

Miranda Ballard
Spaghetti Carbonara

Susannah Blake
Nuttty Chocolate &
 Marshmallow Toast
Sticky Fried Bananas on
 Toast
Tuna Melt

Tamsin Burnett-Hall
Chickpea, Lemon & Mint
 Soup
Pan-fried Caribbean
 Bananas
Smoked Mackerel & Bulgur
 Wheat Salad

Maxine Clark
Olive Oil & Garlic
 Bruschetta
Tomato & Garlic Bruschetta
Tomatoey Green Beans with
 Onion & Fennel Seeds
Zabaglione

Linda Collister
Bang Bang Chicken
Cinnamon Toast

Ross Dobson
Baked Lemon Pudding
Lemony Mushrooms on
 Toast
Lime Pickle & Vegetable
 Biryani
Pan Plum Crumble
Spaghetti with Chilli &
 Courgettes
Swiss Chard & White Bean
 Soup
Warm Pasta Salad with
 Tuna

Silvano Franco
White Spaghetti

Tonia George
Bircher Muesli
Chicken Avgolemono
Pea, Smoked Ham & Mint
 Soup

Nicola Graimes
Bubble & Squeak Patties
Mozzarella & Tuna
 Quesadilla
Strawberry Sundaes

Rachel Anne Hill
Cheat's Cherry Brulée
Cheat's Mini Pizzas
Tuna Pasta Salad

Jennifer Joyce
Chicken Noodle Soup
Corned Beef Hash

Jenny Linford
Baked Mushroom & Egg
 Ramekins
Caldo Verde
Cauliflower Potato Curry
Fettunta
Hash Browns
Herbed Crushed Potatoes
Hummus
Mexican Red Rice
Potato, Apple & Onion Hash
Potato Cheese Scones
Sautéed Potatoes with
 Bacon & Garlic
Tzatziki

Caroline Marson
Iced Summer Berries with
 Hot White Chocolate
 Sauce
Pepperoni, Red Pepper &
 Crouton Frittata
Spicy Halloumi &
 Chickpeas

Theo A. Michaels
Smoked Seafood Spaghetti

Annie Nicholls
Pizza with Potatoes

Jane Noraika
Couscous Tabbouleh
Tomato Soup
Tuscan Tomato & Bread
 Salad

Elsa Peterson-Schepelern
Mixed Bean Soup
Tuna & Bean Salad

Louise Pickford
Bagna Cauda
Baked Eggs with Smoked
 Salmon & Chives
Banana Fritters
Carrot, Orange & Cumin
 Dip
Chicken & Lemon Skewers
Frazzled Eggs & Smoked
 Gammon
Lamb in Pita Bread

Melon with Ginger Syrup
Pesto
Quick Vegetable Curry
Rhubarb Compote with
 Yoghurt
Strawberries with Black
 Pepper
Tapenade

Rena Salaman
Fried Meatballs

Jennie Shapter
Chickpea Tortilla
Sun-dried Tomato Frittata

Anne Sheasby
Thrifty Tips

Fiona Smith
Chopped Liver with Zhoug
Sautéed Greens

Linda Tubby
Fresh Fried Trout

Fran Warde
Beefburgers
Field Mushroom Tortilla
French Toast & Fried
 Tomatoes
Honeyed Chicken Wings
Prawn Curry
Rice Noodle Salad with
 Prawns
Vegetable Noodle Stir-fry

Laura Washburn
Breakfast Burrito
Cauliflower with Anchovies
Ham & Egg Breakfast
 Quesadilla

Lindy Wildsmith
Scotch Pancakes

picture credits

Caroline Arber
Pages 46, 84, 92

Martin Brigdale
Pages 8, 10, 18, 30, 133

Peter Cassidy
Pages 2, 5, 31, 32, 41, 42, 62,
72, 87, 91, 96, 105, 113, 122

Vanessa Davies
Page 69

Nicki Dowey
Page 134

Gus Filgate
Pages, 34, 35

Tara Fisher
Page 6

Jonathon Gregson
Pages 12

Richard Jung
Back cover; Pages 45, 83,
126

Mowie Kay
Front cover

William Lingwood
Pages 4, 49, 130, 137

Diana Miller
Page 114

David Munns
Page 128

Steve Painter
Pages 70, 80

William Reavell
Pages 53, 57, 124, 138

Yuki Sugiara
Pages 37, 38

Debi Treloar
Pages 9, 76

Ian Wallace
Pages 24, 102, 106

Kate Whittaker
Pages 75, 79

Isobel Wield
Pages 20, 27

Clare Winfield
Pages 16, 23, 28, 95, 99, 100,
109, 110, 117, 118, 121